KNOCKABOUT 12

DAYDREAMS AND CON

NIGHT FEARS

TENTS

PARANOIA
5 Jack Alarum **Graham Higgins**
13 Charlie Chirp **Hunt Emerson**
19 Trumped-up Truisms for Scrambled Eggheads **Mike Matthews**
25 The House Next Door **Peter Rigg**

KNOCKABOUT COMICS
30 Encyclopedia of Babies **Daniel Goossens**
   (translated and lettered by Gilbert Shelton)
35 Fat Freddy's Cat **Gilbert Shelton**
36 The Freak Brothers **Gilbert Shelton**
38 International Motoring Tips **Gilbert Shelton**
39 That Awful Borgia Pope **Eddie Campbell**
43 Calculus Cat **Hunt Emerson**

CLASSICS
49 Portrait of the Arteest **Greg Irons**
51 Monkey Lust **Greg Irons**

SERIAL
56 The Adventures of Peter Pank **Max**
   (translated by Elias Garcia and Mike Steel)
Title page drawings **Craig Forrester**

Front Cover **Graham Higgins** (aka Pokkettz)

Knockabout # 12 – The Daydream issue. Copyright © 1986 Knockabout Publications and the contributors. Published by Knockabout, Unit 6a Acklam Workshops, 10 Acklam Road, London W10 5QZ. All rights reserved. No part of this book may be reproduced, recorded or transmitted in any form without prior permission of the publisher.
Layout and design: Rian Hughes. Editors: Carol Bennett, Tony Bennett, Hunt Emerson. ISBN 0 86166 044 7.
Dep. Legal: B - 36.884-86
Printed in Spain by JTV Publishing Services.

PARANOIA

Four stories to keep you awake — or to disturb your nightmares. Jack Alarum, by **Graham Higgins** (aka Pokkettz), disturbs both his own dreams and those of unwary travellers. Wars of worms! — **Hunt Emerson,** who claims never to dream, spies on the daydreams and night fears of birds and worms. **Mike Matthews** upends his own dream bucket and finds it not a pretty sight. And **Pete Rigg's** characters demonstrate the dream-like quality of East-West propaganda.
And now — get under your bed.

WANTED!

JOHN SLITBARK
KNOWN AS
JACK ALARUM

Know ye that a REWARD is offer'd for the catcher of said SLITBARK, lately escaped from the Dock of York Assizes by sundry CHYNEES tricks, & charged with MURTHER & the GAMOOT of KNAVERY.

DEAD WILL DO
2000 DUCATS on his BONES

Written & Drawn by Graham (Pokkettz) Higgins · Lettered by H. Emerson. 1986.

A MIST SETTLES ON THE SHORE, LIKE A BLANKET OF DAMP FELT, PRESSED DOWN BY THE GROWING NIGHT....
LURKHARBOUR ¼ mile
THE BOSUN'S NOSE, EH? A SEAFARER'S DIVE IF I'M NOT MISTAKEN!
NOSE
CHOUC!
INN-KEEPER! SCULLION! POT-BOY! A JUG O' SACK, THERE! YER BEST PARAFINO.!!
oh Sir, sir! I beg thee... 'old yer peace!
I'LL PIPE DOWN WHEN I GETS SOME GROG! BEIN' AS HOW I'VE RUN AGROUND IN THIS MORE DEAD THAN ALIVE HOLE, WRECKED WI' THIRST, I'LL PLUNDER YER CELLAR TO PASS ME TIME...
...AND IF I DON'T IT'LL BE YOUR FUNERAL! SERVICE!!
Oh dear lor'.. don't 'ee say they things! If you will, sir, GO NOW!
...ABJECT FEAR... VERY CIVIL OF YOU... BUT THOUGH I BE CORRUPT, VICIOUS AND DEPRAVED, YET AM I FAIR! FETCH ME YER BEST NOSE-PAINT AN' WE'LL SAY N'MORE!
VERY WELL, SIR.... HAVE A POT WI' ME AND I'LL TELL'E A TALE....

'TWAS A YEAR AGO THIS NIGHT, WHEN **LORD LAWKES**, THE SQUIRE OF **LURKHARBOUR**, AND HIS CRONIES GATHERED ON YONDER SHORE - INTENT ON VILLAINY!

....THE SEA BOILED THAT NIGHT, AND THE BLOOD FROZE, AND SOON THEY ESPIED A TOPSAIL BUCKIN' AND KICKIN' LIKE A LORD ON THE GALLOWS....

.... THEY LURED HER IN, MISTER, BREAKIN' HER BREASTBONE ON THE ROCKS OFF SNATTLES HEAD! POOR LOST SOULS!...

...'TWERE A SHIP OF FOOLES, SIR, ON A GOODWILL MISSION FROM NAPLES....

....LIKE MANY A GOOD ACT BEFORE 'EM, THEY DIED ON THE BOARDS, SIR...

LORD LAWKES 'AD 10,000 DUCATS OFF THAT 'ULK! AND, 'TIS SAID THAT ON THIS NIGHT THE MOST VILE AND LOATHSOME THINGS... 'ORRIBLE, UNMENTIONABLE THINGS WILL COME ASHORE!!!...

10,000 DUCATS??!

YE MEAN... MARINERS' UNDERTHINGS?
NOZUR! NO! FOOLES..! LOOKIN' FER THEIR MONEY! NOW GO, sir, for pity's...
GIVE ME PAUSE TO THINK!
GET ME A LANTHORN AND A BOX O'LUCIFERS!! WHERE'LL I FIND THIS LAWKES?!
HMM! A DUDE TAVERN...
YE WHALERS PROP. FOR ROBT MARLEY
GIMME A BOWL O'BRANDY AND A HANDFUL O' THEY FINE JAMAICY CHEROOTS!!
WANTED
...AND- ...psssssstt... C'MERE...
WHISPER IN JACK'S EAR, MISTER... WHERE DO I FIND SQUIRE LAWKES?
CHO! PUT UP YA BLOODCLAT GUN MON-ME 'AVE BIN THROUGH THIS'T'ING ONE TIME BEFORE! Y'CAN CHECK OUT TH'SQUIRE IN BACK A'DEH...
TANTIVY TANTIVY! HAHAAA! FEED ME PONY, GEL, FEED ME PONY! SPARE THE ROD AND SPOIL THE SPORT! YOIKS!!
DOOF!
DOOF!

WHA?... MY TRIPES- WHO'S THERE?!
EEEEEEEE
WELL, SINK ME YACHTS... I MUST'VE COME TO THE WRONG PLACE! I WAS TOLD SQUIRE LAWKES WUZ A CUNNY-SEWER OF EXOTIC PLEASURES...
...er... That's so....
PFUH! WHERE I COME FROM, SUCH SHENNANIGANS AS THIS ARE CONSIDERED BARELY PECADILLOS! I KNOW WHERE Y'CAN FIND A "DIVERSION" THAT IS TRULY Exotique IF YE CATCH MY MEANIN'...
Harumph!... BE OFF, NOW, GIRL!...
THANK'EE SQUIRE... I BIN ON ME KNEES ALL DAY...
NOW, JACKANAPES- YOU HAVE A PROPOSITION?.?
FER TONIGHT ONLY I CAN OFFER YOU A RARITY SUCH THAT, WERE YOU TO RELATE IT, NONE WOULD BELIEVE YOU!...
is SHE.... ACCOMODATIN'?..
THEY ARE MOST EXPERT IN THEIR TRADE, MILORD, AND EVERY ONE COSTUMED AND DYING TO PRESS THEIR HANDS ON YEW!
Snurk HOW MUCH, YE RASCAL, YE?
10,000 DUCATS FOR ENOUGH NOVELTY TO LAST YER LIFETIME, SQUIRE! COME, DISCREET-LIKE, TO THE BOSUN'S NOSE AT MIDNIGHT!
BUT... I CAN SEE YE'RE IN A STATE O'MANHOOD AT THE PROSPECT!.. GIRL! MORE STRAW FOR HIS LORDSHIP!
Sigh YES, SIR...

OH BOTTY! OH DRAWERS! AREN'T I THE VERY LAD!..
LURKHARBOUR (A GOODLY WAY)
"WHAT A SIZE WHAT A SIZE!" ..Hurr Hurr!..
LURKHARBOUR (A GOOD LEAGUE HENCE)
LURKHARBOUR KEEP GOING
ME DEAR... YOU AIN'T SEEN NOTHIN' YET!..
THE OILY SLAP AND LICK OF THE SEA ON A COLD NEAP-TIDE NIGHT....
IN THE FOG OFFSHORE, A THING BREAKS THE SURFACE.... THEN ANOTHER....
MUFFLED VOICES CARRY OVER THE SHORE AND ARE LOST IN THE MIST.... FOOLES VOICES!..
SPUT!
Caramba Mia It's-a FREEZIN'-A COLD in here, guy!
'Ey, you think-a this is cold? You wanna meet-a my momma-in-law!
'Eh-look-a dis SUIT! Is-a RUIN!
Say, who wassa DRIVIN' da boat, is-a what I wanna know!
When we getta da Money, I gonna have one big bam-BEANO!
HOLD HARD, YE SWABS! YE'RE LOOKIN' FER SQUIRE LAWKES?
Si! Si!
At'sa guy!
WELL HE AIN'T HERE!
AWWWWW!
BUT I CAN SHOW YE WHERE TO FIND 'IM!
YAAAAAY!
Lead on Mac-a-Duff!
IT'LL COST YE...er... 5000 DUCATS!
AWWWW!
...BUT, SINCE YE'RE ALSO PAYIN' EXPENSES, I'LL STAND YEZ ALL A DRINK!
YAAAAAAY!
Prego! What's-a Scam, Sam?

WALK THIS WAY, GENTS, 'N' DO AS I SAY!
If I could walk-a that way....
SHH!
IN THE BOSUN'S NOSE...
LANDLORD, LOCK YERSELF IN THE CELLAR AND STICK CORKS IN YER EARS, IF YOU PLEASE... I'M EXPECTIN' VISITORS! NOW BE OFF!
THANK'EE SQUIRE... I BEEN ON ME KNEES ALL EVENIN'...
GOOD MILORD! ARE YE PREPARED?
I HAVE ME MONEY IF THAT'S WHAT YE MEAN.
I MEANT ARE YE READY FOR THE...ah...ENTERTAINMENTS? CASH-ON-DELIVERY, SEZ I, THE MASTER OF THE REVELS! ARE YE SITTIN' COMFORTABLE, LIKE? THEN WE'LL....
...BEGIN!!
...AND NOW.... THE END IS NEAR... ...AND SO I FACE...
....THE FINAL...
LAVVERLY TUNE...
CURTAIN!!

STEADY, BOY, STEADY.... DON'T FORGET TO FEED ME PONY, MOTHER....
FOOLES RUSH IN....
BAN-A-ZAI!
...AND MIND YE SAVE ME 'IS JACKET!
SALAMI MIA!
'EH-SPATCHINI! MAKE-A WITH THA BANANS!
Tell-a me... how-a you make a Venetian blind?
Like-a this-and-a this!
Boom-a Boom!
VERY WELL, ME JOLLY BOYS...FLASH YOUR CASH AND WE'LL BE ALL FOUR-SQUARE!
CLOMPCLOMPCLOMP!
CHINK!
LANDLORD! IT'S A DRINK FER THE HOUSE!!
YE WOULDN'T HAPPEN TO KEEP THEY FINE JAMAICY CHEROOTS?....
RIGHT AWAY, SIR! I HAVEN'T DONE SUCH TRADE SINCE LADY DAY!
THE END

by HUNT EMERSON
Charlie CHIRP
the Tweeting Twerp!
OK, WORM! COME OUT OF THERE AND TAKE YOUR PUNISHMENT LIKE A WORM!!
NOT LIKELY!
SEEDS
YEAH-COME ON OUT! I'M NOT EVEN A WORM-EATING BIRD... (I eat seeds) AND I DEMAND IT!
WHY?
I LIKE WATCHING OTHER BIRDS TEARING WORMS TO BITS!
YOU BASTARD!
SEEDS
OK YOUZ BIRDS.... EES I, FERDINAND BERDINANDO, ZE BANDITO BIRDO! HAND OVER YOUR WORMS!
BLIMEY TWEET!
TUFF LUCK! I DON'T HAVE ANY WORMS! I'VE GOT ONE TREE'D IN THIS HOLE, BUT IT WON'T COME OUT.... OTHERWISE-ZERO!
IZZAT SO?
OK! STAND BACK YOUZ BIRDS! I GET ZIS WORM OUT PRONTO, SI!!
COME OUT, YOU DINGBLAMTWEET WORM, YOU! VAMOS! SCRAM!! AVANTE!!!
BLAM!

-ONE-

-TWO-

munch
MY FAVOURITE IS STEAMED SEED, BUT IT'S OK RAW, TOO...
I CAN'T EAT SEED, YOU KNOW... ONLY WORMS...
HEY BIRDS! I BRING HELP IN THE SHAPE OF THIS STROLLING CRAZY SCIENTIST-AND-PHILOSOPHER!
CRAZY?
HE'D HAVE TO BE CRAZY TO TALK TO BIRDS, WOULDN'T HE!...
YEAH...S'POSE SO... LISTEN, PROF... HERE'S THE PROBLEM...
SNORE
PATIENTLY, THEY IMPRESS UPON THE STROLLING CRAZY SCIENTIST-AND-PHILOSOPHER'S BRAIN THE ELEMENTS OF THE PROBLEM!!
TWEET TWEET TWEETY TWEET
...AND NOW, YOU SEE, THE WORM IS SOUND ASLEEP!
SI!
ASLEEP?? FORTUNATELY I HAVE HERE MY LATEST CARDBOARD AND STRING INVENTION.... Snurkle..
HEAT-SEEKING DREAM T.V.!! WITH THIS MACHINE WE CAN SPY ON WHAT THE WORM IS DREAMING!
HE IS CRAZY, ISN'T HE!
...AS A CONKER!
Blimey O'Rielly! Nearly no room for me in this frame!

-THREE-

OK! SWITCH ON! WHERE IS THE CRITTER?...
I want my din-din!
Relax, Charlie Chirp-ees soon come!
ZZZz
AHA! CONTACT! HOWZIT LOOK? WHAT'S THE WORM DREAMING OF?!?
Ancient Bird Curse
SKRAMBLO DOKBLIT CONDILIAX!!! IT'S DREAMING OF EATING ME!! HOW DARE IT!?! THIS IS SEDITION!!!
yum yum yum
BEEP BEEP BEEP BEEP BEEP BEEP
LEMME AT IT! I'LL TEAR IT OUT WITH ME BARE BEAK!
HOLD ON! WAIT! DON'T EXCITE YOURSELF!
IT'S PERFECTLY NATURAL.... EVERYTHING DREAMS OF EATING OR BEING EATEN....
WATCH - I'LL TURN IT ON THEM SEEDS.... SEE WHAT THEY'RE DREAMING!
CHOMP
CHEW
MUNCH
BEEP BEEP BEEP
Hey!!
EXCUSE ME, SEÑOR... IZ WORKS ON SLEEPING BIRDS TOO, SI?
OH, SI-ER... YES!
WALLOP!
THERE YOU ARE - EATING OR BEING EATEN! IN THIS CASE YOUR FRIEND DREAMS OF BEING EATEN UP BY GUILT...
HE'S NO FRIEND OF OURS... CHARLIE CHIRP DON'T HAVE ANY FRIENDS...
GUILT
ZZZZ
BEEP BEEP BEEP

-FOUR-

- FIVE -

I'M GETTING FED UP WITH ALL THIS- I WANT MY WORM!
Si! AND I ALSO WANTS HIS WORM!
OKAY OKAY....
YEAH- C'MON MAESTRO- GET DAT WOIM WOKE!
...er...LETS SEE WHAT ITS DREAMING NOW, EH? gulp
ZEEP ZEEP ZEEP
"ANOTHER EATING DREAM! AND IF I'M NOT MISTAKEN, THIS ONE'S ALSO RATHER NAUGHTY! FAR TOO NAUGHTY FOR YOU, MY FINE FEATHERED FRIENDS...."
...SO YOU'D BETTER NOT LOOK! COME ON, NOW....ALL COVER YOUR EYES AT ONCE!...
TWEET! TWEET TWEET! HEY GERROFF!! WAAAH!! TWEET!
TWEET TWEET! OI! TWEET!! I WANNA SEE!! LET ME SEE!! TWEET! TWEET! TWEET
SKWAAK!
I SAY...LOOK OVER THERE... ISN'T THAT?..
GOOD GOD - SO IT IS!
DEAR OH DEAR... HE'S BEEN OVERWORKING.
YEEES... I DARESAY...
MAYBE IF WE ALL SHOUT DOWN THE WORMHOLE...
...COME ON THEN, ALL YOU BIRDS! ALL SHOUT TOGETHER...
SHAME...I HAD HIM EARMARKED FOR A DIRECTORHSIP.
WAKE UP WORM!!
THE END

TRUMPED-UP TRUISMS for SCRAMBLED EGGHEADS

As narrated to MIKE MATTHEWS ©'86 by DOKTOR CHESTER (sic) CHOAK, M.D. (MAD DOCTOR). Who claims: "I GOT MY DEGREE FROM THE 'SORE-BONE UNIVERSITY'. THEY JUST LEAVE 'EM LYING AROUND IN A DRAWER..! I MEAN, ANYONE CAN JUST TAKE ONE..! WHADDAYA EXPECT..?! HONESTLY...?! FROM A DOCTOR...?!!"

SO, IT'S TALES of **DAYDREAMS** AND **NIGHTFEARS** YER WANTIN' eh?! IDLE DOZY DREAMS of **IDYLLIC** SUMMER REVERIE... OR PLUNGES INTO THE **DARK** PITS of **SWEAT-SOAKED FEAR, HORROR,** AND **DESPAIR**?!!

WELL, I GOT 'EM ON MY MENU: I'LL GIVE YOU A PRESCRIPTION FOR A RECIPE THAT'LL WORK WONDERS..! SO, HERE, MY CURIOUS PATIENT, STARVED OF UNDERSTANDING, HUNGRY FOR A CURE-ALL FOR ALL YOUR ILLS... I'LL SERVE UP SOME TASTY MEDICINE THAT'LL FILL YOUR BELLY AND FIRE YOUR BRAIN... OR VICE-VERSA...

NO MATTER... NOW HOLD STILL... I JUST HAVE TO..er... PERFORM A SLIGHT REMOVAL OF YOUR BRAIN..! DON'T WORRY..! I'M A DOCTOR! HEH-HEH! SNURK!

PSYCHIATRISTS COOKBOOK — HOW TO CURE NUTS, FRUITCAKES, DINGLEBERRIES and FROTHING LOONS BEFORE FRYING THEM TO A CRISP WITH E.S.T.

C'M'ERE YER LI'L BUGGER — GRUNT..! SSSCHLOOP!!

Ah! HERE IT IS! YOUR **BRAIN**! THE BODY'S MOST DELICATE ORGAN!!

OOPS! SQUISH — AND ONE OF THE SLIPPIEST!

er.. JUST A SLIGHT MISHAP..! heh-heh! WON'T TAKE A MOMENT TO RECTIFY..! C'MERE YOU SNOTTY BLOB!!!

FIRSTLY TO SECURE THE BRAIN TO THE, uh, OPERATING TABLE... GRUNT! BANG! BANG! BANG!

THEN, WITH THIS SPECIAL MIND-MICROSCOPE WE EXAMINE IT! BZZZZT!

DON WANNA! SPLAP! BLAP! SPLOP!

POP! SQUEEK! SPOING! ZIP! FZZST! TWANG! BLIP! POP!

19

NOW THE 'MIND-MICROSCOPE' PROBES *DEEP* INTO THE *HIDDEN RECESSES* OF YOUR...er...*MIND* AND TRANSFORMS THE POLYZONG LATERAL WAVES INTO IMAGES, AND LOTS MORE *GOBBLEDEGOOK* TECHNICAL STUFF WHICH I CAN'T BE BOTHERED TO *MAKE UP*. ANYWAY, YOU *GET* THE PICTURE...

SO: WHAT DO WE HAVE *HERE* ?! Ah, YES... A TYPICAL "IF I *RULED* THE *WORLD*" DAYDREAM...! heh-heh-heh..! NO MORE *POVERTY*! NO MORE *INJUSTICE*! ALL IS *PEACE* AND *TRANQUILITY*... *EVERYONE* IS *NICE*! JUST LIKE *YOU*..!

WELL, BUSTER, A *QUICK FLICK* O'THE *WRIST* AND *BAM*! *HUNGER*! *POVERTY*! *REAL LIFE*!

AND THERE *YOU* ARE, *SUFFERING* WITH ALL THE *REST*! WITH AN *ACHING BELLY* AND *FESTERING* IN *HOPELESS DESPAIR*. ONE OF *MILLIONS*.

WHO *CARES* ?!

I SAID *WHO CARES* ?!?

I SAID...

Oh, FORGET IT...!

Ah; SO, YOU COUNTER *THAT* WITH A QUICK 'RAMBO' MACHO-MAN FANTASY, EH ?!/

'*WAR IS FUN*!'

WOW! JUST *LOOK* AT YOU MOWING *DOWN* THEM *COMMIES*! AIN'T IT *LUCKY* THEY'RE *ALL* SUCH *BAD SHOTS* ?! GITSOME!! *BODY COUNT*!! *WEAPONS SYSTEMS*!! *GUNS 'N' AMMO*!!! ALL IS *FARE* IN *LOVIN*' *WAR*.

NERRR! DOINK! YADDA YADDA!

Now HERE'S SOMETHING *CLOSER* TO THE *TRUTH*... YOU'RE JUST *ONE* OF *MILLIONS*... *CANNON FODDER*... YOU'RE NOT *SURE* WHERE YOU ARE... YOU'RE *OUT* OF *AMMUNITION* AND HAVEN'T *EATEN* IN THREE *DAYS*...

YOU'VE BEEN *HIT* IN THE *BELLY* AND IT *HURTS LIKE HELL* BUT YOU'RE *TOO SCARED* TO *CRY OUT* BECAUSE YOU *DON'T KNOW* IF YOUR *POSITION'S BEEN OVERRUN*...

YOU *DON'T KNOW* IF THE *RUMOURS* ARE *TRUE* ABOUT WHAT THEY *DO* TO *WOUNDED* AND *PRISONERS*...

YOU DON'T *KNOW* WHAT'S *GOING ON*... YOU *DON'T KNOW*...

Ah! '*DREAM GIRL*!' I WAS *WAITING* FOR HER TO POP UP! *IMPOSSIBLY BEAUTIFUL*, ALWAYS *COOL* AND *HAPPY* AND *UNDERSTANDING*... FULL OF *ADORATION*, *LOVE* AND *CONCERN*... *GOOD FUN* AND *FUNNY*, ALWAYS *SMELLS NICE* AND LOOKS *GORGEOUS*...

WHAT A *PITY* SHE *DOESN'T EXIST*!

AND IF SHE *DID*, YOU THINK SHE'D *SETTLE* FOR *YOU* ?!

HA!!

HEE HEE HEE! HERE'S THE *NIGHTMARE* MONSTER FEMALE YOU *DREAD*... A *SHREIKING VAIN LYING UGLY HARPIE*: ALWAYS *MOANING* AND *CRYING* AND *COMPLAINING*!

~~YAKH!~~

NOW SHE *DOES* EXIST; AND WHAT'S *MORE*, *THAT'S* WHAT YOU'LL *END UP* WITH, YOU *POOR BASTARD*!

AND WILL *THAT* SATISFY HER ?! Oh, *NO*, JACK! SHE'LL *ALWAYS* HAVE A *SNEAKY EYE* OPEN FOR *ANOTHER JERK* WHO SHE CAN *TURN* INTO A *MISERABLE WRECK*.

SO I SUPPOSE YOU'VE GOT *SOMETHIN'* TO *LOOK FORWARD* TO: NAMELY = IF SHE *DECIDES* TO *PISS OFF* AND *LEAVE* YOU *ALONE*!

ME WANT MONEY!! ME WANT MORE! GRIPE! MOAN! BITCH! YAK YAK!

REPULSIVE WOMOAN — 10 NEW WAYS TO CAUSE AN ARGUMENT! FAT? STINK? UGLY? TAMPONS — ART NEW PMT AND BEAUTY OR STUPID — BE A BITCH — HOW TO BE A TOTAL TWAT

20

ALONE... Ah YES! THAT LEADS TO THE SINGLE INDIVIDUAL... ALONE... SELF-SUFFICIENT... "I DON'T NEED NOBODY!" "I'M O.K. BY MYSELF!" "YESSIREEE!" "I'M FREE!" "FREE TO DO ANYTHING I WANT!" "GO WHERE I WANT!" "WHEN I WANT!" "DON'T NO-ONE ROCK MY BOAT!" "I'M ON MY WAY!" "ME!" "JUST ME! AND NO-ONE ELSE!" "UH-HUH!" "YES SIR!!!" **BUT...**

"GO FOR IT!! GET THERE!!! $UCCE$$ FAME!!! RESPECT!"

BUT... ALONE IS LONELY... WHEN YOU'RE ALONE AND WANT SOMEONE ELSE... NEED SOMEONE ELSE TO SHARE YOUR LIFE WITH... WHEN JUST *YOU* JUST AIN'T ENOUGH! NO! IT JUST AIN'T! SHIT! ALL THOSE BILLIONS OF PEOPLE IN THE WORLD AND NOT ONE TO TALK TO... AND YOU ONLY NEED ONE..! JUST ONE! SOMEONE SPECIAL!

SUFFER THE CREEPING FLESH AGONY OF EXISTENTIAL DESPAIR. BOO-HOO! "I NEED SOMEBODY!" UH-UH BUSTER! NO WAY, JOSÉ! YOU MADE IT, YOU EAT IT! SUFFER!

WHAT?! YOU COUNTER WITH A QUICK ONE OFF THE WRIST? A MUCKY MASTURBATORY FANTASY? OH, WELL... HAUL IT OUT AND GET IT UP...HERE SHE IS, BOYS! 'MISS EVER-READY ORGASM'! A SENSUOUS SEX-SIREN SLUT! ORAL, ANAL OR ANYWAY YOU WANT IT! ANYTIME, ANYWHERE, ANYHOW! MADE UP OF RETOUCHED 4-COLOUR DOTS PRINTED ON PAPER! SHE'S CHEAP! BUY HER IN ANY ADULT MAGAZINE EMPORIUM OF POPULAR CULTURE! SNORT! SLURP!

"I LOVE IT!" says TEAZA OF BELGRAVIA!

...er... HOW COME THE SKIN-MAG LADIES NEVER MENTION CONTRACEPTION... OR V.D... OR WORRYING WHETHER HER BOYFRIEND'S GONNA BUST IN WITH A BUTCHER KNIFE..?! OR HER MOTHER WITH A HEART ATTACK..?! HOW COME IT'S NEVER... YOU KNOW... THE SAME..?! HOW COME YOU ALWAYS WONDER 'AFTERWARDS'... WHETHER SHE 'ENJOYED' IT... WHETHER YOU 'ENJOYED' IT... WHETHER IT WAS WORTH THE TROUBLE... WHY THE FUCK YOU BOTHER?!!

AAOHWHHHH!! UH! ARE YOU ALRIGHT?! OUCH! SQUELCH! SHLOOP! SLURP! SPLAP! SLP! DON'T STAIN THE SHEETS! OH GOD! DON'T DO THAT! SORRY! UH! DID YOU COME?! er... I DUNNO! AH!

HEE HEE HEE!! I'M ENJOYING THIS! WE'RE REALLY PLUMBING THE DEPTHS OF NITTY-GRITTINESS, REACHING NEW HIGHS AND LOWS IN OUR ETERNAL QUEST FOR TRUTH!

WHAT?! YOU WANT TO KNOW THE TRUTH, TOO?!! WELL THAT'S A FUCKIN' LIE FOR A START, JOHN!!! DO ME A FAVOUR!

BACK AFTER THE COMMERCIAL BREAK

YES, FOLKS; **TRUTH** CAN BE FOUND HIDING IN **DREAMS** AND **FEARS**... IF YOU WANT TO FIND IT...! AND MOST PEOPLE DON'T! THEY WANT THE COMFORT OF LIES. IT'S EASIER! I MEAN... WHY STRUGGLE AND SUFFER WHEN IT'S SOOO MUUUCH EEEASIER TO... HAVE IT EASY?! WHY? TELL ME WHY!!! FOR PERSONAL PRIDE? WILL THAT PAY THE RENT?! FOR MORALS AND ETHICS? WILL THEY SCORE SOME EASY LAYS?! BECAUSE YOU WANNA BE REMEMBERED AS A GOOD GUY? WELL, SHIT, YOU AIN'T GONNA BE AROUND TO APPRECIATE THE ACCLAIM EVEN IF YOU GET IT!

LISTEN, HONEY... DON'T CRY! I CAN SAY ALL THIS SHIT BECAUSE... WELL... TO BE HONEST... I DON'T EXIST! I CAN NEVER BE THE BARREL OF DELUDED BULLSHIT HUMANS ARE BECAUSE I'M JUST LINES ON PAPER...! INK ON PULPED WOOD! A CARTOON CHARACTER!
GOD FORBID I SHOULD BE YOU!
I'M HAPPY AS I AM; THANK YOU!
COMIC STRIP INK
JUST SPLOSH IT ON: CHARACTERS POP UP FROM NOWHERE!
I MEAN, TAKE THE... ahem: 'ARTIST' (I USE THAT TERM FOR WANT OF A MORE FITTING DESCRIPTION THAT DOES NOT, AS YET, EXIST, I'M AFRAID!) WHO'S 'DRAWING' ME NOW: YOU THINK YOU'RE SCREWED UP? JEEZ, HE IS A MESS!
I AIN'T NEVER SEEN SUCH A SCREWED UP, SELF-DELUDED INDIVIDUAL! MY GOD! THE LIES HE TELLS HIMSELF, AND MAKES HIMSELF BELIEVE! IF IT WASN'T SO PATHETIC HE'D BE HILARIOUS!
HE'S SO TANGLED UP IN KNOTS OF POINTLESS HATE, UNGROUNDED FEAR, IMPOSSIBLE AMBITION, ALL-ROUND BASIC UGLY STUPIDITY AND HIS OWN PERVERSE IDEAS ABOUT BEAUTY AND GOD KNOWS WHAT THAT I DOUBT IF HE'LL EVER STRAIGHTEN OUT TO BECOME A NORMAL HUMAN BEING, YOU KNOW, A USEFUL MEMBER OF SOCIETY WITH A STEADY JOB, HIS OWN HOME AND A WIFE AND KIDS.
IT'S NOT TRUE!! CAN I HELP IT IF I'M RIGHT AN' EVERYONE ELSE IS WRONG?!!
DEAD COMMON MANCUNIAN ACCENT.
SHIT! IF I WAS HIM I'D SLIT MY FUCKIN' THROAT!
COME 'ERE! I'LL BLEEDIN' KILL YOU!!!
YAHAH! CAN'T TAKE IT! THE TRUTH HURTS, BABY! SORT YOURSELF OUT BEFORE YOU START PREACHING TO THE UNCONVERTABLE YA DAFT BASTARD!
HEY! BADLY-DRAWN BLACK'N WHITE SCRIBBLE! DO YOU BELIEVE IN GOD?!
NOW HOW CAN A TWO-DIMENSIONAL IMAGE BELIEVE IN GOD?!
er... WHY?
'COZ YER JUST MET 'IM! SHAZOOOM! ONE MIGHTY FLICK OF MY BRUSH AND I CAN CHANGE YOU INTO ANYTHING I WANT! BEGONE UGLY CLOWN! I DESIRE A BUXOM WENCH TO SHED HER KNICKERS! SO BE IT!!!
EEEK!!
THINK YOU'RE BLEEDING CLEVER; DON'T YOU, YOU ALL-POWERFUL GIT! WELL I DEFY YOUR WANKY BRUSH-STROKES! MY NUDENESS SHALL NOT INSULT THE EYEBALLS OF YOUR VIEWERS!
RIIIP!!
RIIIP!

WELL PISS OFF THEN. JEEZ, THESE LITTLE CARTOON CHARACTERS JUST GET CARRIED AWAY...!

SOMETIMES YOU JUST GOTTA KILL 'EM OFF..!

AAAAGH!
LET ME OUT..!

GOD I'M BORED..!
WHAT CAN I DO NOW?
I'VE JUST MURDERED MY LEADING ACTOR IN MY EPIC TRAGEDIC DISCOURSE UPON THE NATURE OF DREAMS...!
SO WHAT DO I DRAW NOW?!
WHAT CAN I DO..?
I GOTTA DO SOMETHING..!
BUT WHAT..?
WHAT?!
WHAT..?

BINGO! I KNOW! I'LL DO...

DAN MANIAC

DETECTIVE OF DOOM

Beyond LAW. Beyond REASON. Beyond the Eternal Powers of the Infiniteness of... er... Everything! Dan's battle against Crime is a never-ending War.

But...even Dan Maniac must sleep. Yes, even HE must sometimes rest his weary wartorn limbs in exhausted slumber between cases. Even he must attempt to sleep, perchance to DREAM...

But, even when sleeping, Dan always keeps at least one eye open. Watching for it.

And in Dan's dreams, Peace, for once, prevails. Vista's of panoramas unsullied by the prescence of Humanity and its accompanying sordid criminal activities. As Vultures whirl lazily overhead, Dung Beetles happily roll along their aromatic cargoes, as frolicsome Octopii play among the daffodils.

Dan wallows in the *bliss-riddled guts* of his *idyll*. His *tommygun* sunbathes in lazy contentment.

It's *gleaming oiled surface* soaking up a *healthy tan*.

SUDDENLY a hollow thunder heaves into the reverie.

To his *consternation* Dan sees a *City* rise *around* him in *all* its *rancid glory*. Filthy, noisy and teeming. Spilling its *human detritus* to *infest* its *already stinking streets* and *alleyways*.

An soon...there it was. The *hum* and *horror* of a *City* surrounded him. To his *dismay* Dan inhaled the *stench-laden* flavours of its *evil prescence*.

He *braced* himself for the *inevitable onslaught* of *trouble*.

It would *come*. It always *did*.

Here it comes. Rising like a *cloud* of *doom*, advancing on *Dan* with *terrible certainty*. It's *shadow* enveloping him like a *shroud*.

DAN!! I'M GOING TO GET YOU!!

Dan reacted in *time-honoured* fashion. But to *no avail*. The 'Creature' lumbered inexorably onward. Nothing could *halt* its *murderous assault*.

WELL GET THIS YOU GROSS GARGANTUAN GEEK!!

RATTA-TATTA-TAT!

THE TOMMYGUN OF JUSTICE DOESN'T STOP YOU?! WHAT... WHO ARE YOU?!!

YES! DAN HAD FOUGHT AND LOST WITH THE MONSTER FROM THE DEPTHS OF HIS OWN WORST NIGHTMARES!

HI! YUP! IT'S ME!

PUNT!

WELL... -CRUNCH!- THAT'S THAT! -SCHOMP!- I GOTTA GO NOW!

SO BYE-BYEEE! SEE YOU IN MY DREAMS... OR IN YOUR NIGHTMARES!

Night night, Sleep tight, Don't let the bed-bugs bite

24

THE HOUSE NEXT DOOR

EMMA · OLGA · SASHA · IVAN · JOE · BUCK · LAURA · NADINE

HI! I'M LAURA! WE GOTTA REAL PRETTY HOUSE AN' ALL, Y'ALL, BUT MAH HUSBAND, JOE —THAT'S HIM RIGHT THERE—

—WELL, LET'S JUST SAY I'D LIKE IT A WHOLE LOT BETTER IF HE'D GIT ALONG WITH THE GUY NEXT DOOR! TAKE A LOOK IN THE BACKYARD, AN' YOU'LL SEE WHUT I MEAN....

GODDAMMIT, IVAN! GIT OUTTA MAH BACKYARD, WILLYA?

I'M NOT EVEN IN YOUR STUPID GARDEN! WELL QUIT LOOKIN' AT IT, OK?

WHAT DO I WANT TO LOOK AT IT FOR? I'VE ENOUGH TO DO IN MY OWN GARDEN!

AW, YOU'RE MAKIN' ME CRY! LOOKS TO ME LIKE YOUR WIFE HAS TO DO IT ALL! NOW LISTEN! YOU LEAVE OLGA OUT OF IT!

MAKE ME! COME ON, BIG-SHOT, MAKE ME!

I SWEAR, IVAN, YOU'RE AS YELLOW AS A BOXCAR FULL OF BANANAS!

SO? YOU'VE GOT A BANANA FOR A BRAIN!

25

HEY! QUIT BUGGIN' MAH POPPA, MISTER!

JOE! BUCK! C'MON IN, BOYS, THERE'S FOOD ON THE TABLE! LET'S CHOW DOWN AN' PIG OUT!

YOU SHOULDN'T PROVOKE HIM, YOU KNOW, IVAN. IT ONLY MAKES THINGS WORSE!

I'M SICK OF PEOPLE BLAMING ME ALL THE TIME! I'LL HAVE TO THINK OF SOMETHING....

SO....

MY PIGGY! MY PIGGY!

DON'T TELL ME! I HAVE TO PAWN MY CHESS SET AGAIN!

SHUT UP YOU TWO! WE NEED EVERY COPECK FOR THIS PLAN!

WHAT IS IT THIS TIME, IVAN? NEW BARBED WIRE FOR THE GARDEN!?

NO, OLGA! THIS TIME WE PLAY THEM AT THEIR OWN GAME!

WHAT I NEED IS A NEW IMAGE!

SOME TIME LATER....

THAT'S IVAN BACK AGAIN. HE'D BETTER KEEP THAT MOSKVITCH OFF OF OUR DRIVEWAY, OR I'LL —

— NO, IT'S OK, HE'S —

VRRRRRRRRMMMM!!!!

26

"HEY! LAURA! GET A LOAD OF THIS!"

"HI DOLL! WHAT'S FOR TEA?"

"HOW D'YA LIKE THAT GUY! STILL, I GOTTA ADMIT, OL' IVAN LOOKS KINDA CUTE IN THAT NEAT SUIT!"

"HEY! WHAT IF LAURA THINKS SO TOO?"

"HOW DO I KNOW WHUT SHE'S DREAMIN' ABOUT?"

THAT NIGHT...

27

HELL, IVAN— COMMUNISM, CAPITALISM, WHO GIVES A PECK OF POSSUM SHIT ANYHOW, HUH?
DEAD RIGHT, JOE! LET'S GET ON THAT BEACH AND FORGET THE WHOLE THING!
LAURA, I SUPPOSE YOU AND OLGA MUST'VE GOT PRETTY FED UP OF US TWO FIGHTING ALL THE TIME...
YUP!
WELL GET THIS, HONEY— ME AN' IVAN ARE BUDDIES NOW, AN' WE'RE THROUGH FIGHTIN', Y'HEAR? . . . — HONEY? YOU ASLEEP? HEY! WAKE UP! — YOU'RE DREAMIN'—
POP!
—YOU'RE DREAMIN' OF THAT SLAVIC SLOB, AIN'T YOU? AIN'T YOU? C'MON WAKE YOUR ASS UP!
NEXT MORNING...
HEY, IVAN! WHAT HAPPENED TO THE ELTON JOHN OUTFIT?
THAT'S ME, JOE. I TOLD HIM HE WAS FAR TOO FAT TO EVEN DREAM OF DRESSING LIKE THAT!
HAW! HAW! HELL, OLGA, YOU GAVE OL' IVAN HERE ONE HELLUVA RUDE AWAKENIN', HUH?!!
AND YOU KNOW SOMETHIN' FOLKS? I KNOW JUST HOW HE FEELS!
PETER Rigg
THE END

KNOCKABOUT COMICS

Ever wondered why Hollywood is home to so many drunk babies? **Daniel Goossens'** Baby Encyclopedia devotes a chapter to providing answers. Goossens is a regular contributor to French humour magazine Fluide Glacial, and can stand on his head. That cat, those familiar clowns and several inebriated connoisseurs are the heads stepped on by **Gilbert Shelton** this time. **Eddie Campbell's** strip adds to the sum of human knowledge about that 14th century dynasty, The Borgias. **Hunt Emerson's** black cat, Calculus, and his troublesome T.V. find new depths in household damp, when the sea comes to tea.

FROM THE
ENCYCLOPEDIA OF BABIES
BABIES AND CINEMA

BABIES ARE EXPLOITED IN THE CINEMA BECAUSE THEY ALWAYS EVOKE STRONG EMOTIONS AND EASILY CAPTURE THE VIEWER'S ATTENTION.

ONE SEES IT PARTICULARLY WHEN SOMETHING AS TRAGIC AS THE DEATH OF A BABY IS FILMED. THE DEATH OF A BABY ON THE SCREEN, PARTICULARLY WHEN IT IS A MURDER, IS AN UNENDURABLE SIGHT. TOTALLY UNBEARABLE.

THUS, IN "THE HARPER JOB", FOR INSTANCE, THE SCENE IN WHICH THE BABY IS MURDERED IS INTOLERABLE.

JACQUES BOUDINOT'S NOTE:

A BABY'S COURAGE

IN THE EISENSTEIN FILM "POTEMKIN" THERE IS A SCENE IN WHICH A MOTHER, HIT BY A STRAY SHOT FIRED BY THE POLICE, LETS GO OF HER BABY-CARRIAGE WHICH SHE WAS PUSHING UP THE IMMENSE ODESSA STAIRS, AND THE BABY-CARRIAGE BEGINS TO ROLL DOWN THE STEPS, GAINING SPEED AS IT GOES, FINALLY CRASHING AT THE BOTTOM.
 I HAVE ALWAYS TOLD MYSELF THAT THE BABY WHO PLAYED THAT RÔLE MUST HAVE HAD TREMENDOUS COURAGE.
 IN FACT, THE PART WAS PLAYED BY A STUNT MAN.

WH... WHO ARE YOU? WHAT DO YOU WANT?

NO... YOU CAN'T GO IN THERE... THERE'S NOTHING IN THERE... NOTHING AT ALL...

NOOOOO... GO AWAY... LEAVE US ALONE...

LEAVE HIM ALONE, PLEASE GO.

ENCYCLOPEDIA OF BABIES

LEAVE HIM ALLOONE

NOOOOOO

NOOOOOO

NO... BLACKIE... LISTEN... NO... WAIT...

GO AWAYYYY

TCHT TCHT

BLACKIE... WE CAN WORK IT OUT... I... IT... IT WASN'T ME, BLACKIE... I WASN'T IN ON IT... THEY MADE ME... I...

LEAVE US ALONE

HERE, BLACKIE... IT'S YOUR PART OF THE LOOT... TAKE IT... I... I'VE KEPT IT FOR YOU... I KNEW YOU'D COME BACK... YOU BELIEVE ME, DON'T YOU?... BLACKIE?

PLEASE DON'T HURT HIM

BLACKIE... NO... NO... WAIT... NO

NOOOOOOOOOO

B... BLACKIE... WH... WHO... WHY... B....

TFLP TFLP

B....

B... BLAC... ...BLA....

HAHH HHAHH HH

MURDERER! YOU'VE KILLED HIM!

WH... WHY? B..BL.. WH...

YOU KILLER

WH...WHY... HHH... HH..HH.. UH...

CRACK

CRIMINAL

BLAM

ENCYCLOPEDIA OF BABIES

BEAST, SABOTEUR, POLTROON, JACKANAPES.

SO LONG, HARPER.

THAT WAS TERRIBLE. SIMPLY TERRIBLE.

THE BABY DIDN'T UNDERSTAND WHY.

AT ONE POINT HE ASKS, "WHY, BLACKIE? WHY?"

BUT BLACKIE DOESN'T TELL HIM WHY.

YES YES YES YES YES

THEN HE ASKS WHY DOESN'T BLACKIE TELL HIM WHY.

IN ORDER TO UNDERSTAND WHY THE DEATH OF A BABY IS MORE UNBEARABLE THAN, FOR EXAMPLE, THE DEATH OF AN OLD PERSON, IT SEEMS TO ME ONE MUST COMPARE THE TESTICLES.

IF YOU WILL PERMIT ME, I WOULD LIKE TO SHOW YOU A COMPARATIVE CHART OF THE TESTICLES WHICH I BELIEVE TO BE RELEVANT TO THE SUBJECT.

YES... YES... YES... PLEASE... YES... VERY NICE... YES... LET'S GO ON...

LISTEN, IF YOU DON'T MIND, LET'S RETURN TO OUR DISCUSSION, WHICH WAS ABOUT THE DEATH OF BABIES. MR. GRINGOIRE, YOU HAVE WRITTEN THAT CINEMATIC BABY-DEATHS ARE MORE ACCEPTABLE IF THE BABY IS DRUNK.

THE FIRST THING THAT STRUCK ME WAS THE EXTREME DIFFERENCE BETWEEN THE TEXTURE OF THE SCROTUM OF THE BABY, ON ONE HAND, AND THAT OF THE OLD MAN ON THE OTHER...

YES, BECAUSE THE DRUNKER THE BABY IS, THE LESS THE VIEWER IDENTIFIES WITH HIM.

AHA. COULD YOU EXPLAIN THAT TO US?

I'D LIKE TO ASK THE CAMERAMAN FOR A CLOSE-UP OF THIS, PLEASE.

FURTHERMORE, THE AUDIENCE MAY EVEN *INVEIGH* AGAINST THE BABY, ON THE PRETEXT HE IS DRUNK.

AH YES? BUT FOR WHAT REASON?

AS YOU SEE, THE SCROTUM SKIN IS MUCH MORE DISTENDED IN THE OLD PERSON THAN IT IS IN THE BABY.

TO BE EXACT, THE TESTICLES OF THE BABY ARE LESS DISGUSTING THAN THOSE OF THE OLD MAN.

AND THE MORE THE BABY GOES ABOUT IN THIS STATE OF DRUNKENNESS, THE MORE HATE THE SPECTATOR FEELS, OF THE SAME SORT THAT ENDEAVORS TO BRING ABOUT THE SYMBOLIC UNCONSCIOUS FATHER-MURDER.

REALLY? REALLY? PLEASE TELL US HOW.

ENCYCLOPEDIA OF BABIES

"THAT'S JUST THE WAY IT IS."

"TO SUM IT UP, THE OLD HAVE TWO REASONS MORE FOR COMPLAINT THAN DO BABIES:
1. THE SKIN OF THEIR TESTICLES IS DISTENDED.
2. THEIR DEATH ON SCREEN IS BEARABLE."

"VERY WELL, I WOULD LIKE TO THANK ALL OF YOU FOR YOUR PARTICIPATION, AND I BID YOU FAREWELL UNTIL THE NEXT SHOW."

"QUITE SO, GENTLEMEN, BUT I MUST REMIND YOU OF THE IMPORTANCE OF THE TESTICLES."

"MY FRIENDS... MY FRIENDS... I HAVE BROUGHT YOU HERE TO THIS PLACE OF MAGIC-WORKING....."

"QUEL CRAN"

"...TO SHOW YOU THIS EVENING A MASK... A MASK OF LAUGHTER. A MASK OF LAUGHTER, A MASK FOR LAUGHTER, SO THE PARTY MIGHT LAUGH."

"WHEN HARPER PUTS ON HIS FUNNY MASK, I DESIRED ABOVE ALL AN INTERPRETATION BASED ON LAUGHTER. IT REQUIRED STRONG IMAGERY. SO I STRETCHED OUT THE SCENE AS LONG AS I COULD."

"IMAGES OF PLEASURE, AND A LONG PAN SHOT OF HILARIOUS LAUGHTER"

"THE GUESTS ARE ENJOYING THEMSELVES, AND THAT IS WHAT IS IMPORTANT. THE CAMERA ANGLES BECOME VIOLENT, UNEXPECTED..."

"BUT OVER IN HIS CORNER, BENEATH HIS MASK, PROUDLY, HARPER STANDS THERE, IMPERTURBABLE."

"OR AT LEAST ONE WOULD THINK SO. HE MIGHT BE LAUGHING HIS HEAD OFF, BUT THE MASK HIDES ALL. HE *MASKS* HIS FEELINGS. I WANTED THIS AMBIGUITY."

ENCYCLOPEDIA OF BABIES

Sleeping Beauty

"THEN WHEN HARPER TAKES OFF HIS MASK, YOU SEE THAT HE IS WEEPING BITTERLY. THE SADNESS OF THE CLOWN. I WANTED THIS GAG."

BY MY POWERS, LET THIS CHILD GROW UP TO HAVE THE GIFT OF DANCE.

AH, I CAN SEE IT.

AS FOR ME, I PRONOUNCE THIS CHILD TO BE GIFTED IN THE ART OF READING, THAT SHE MAY BE ACCOMPLISHED.

I THINK I CAN SEE IT.

FOR MY PART, I HEREBY DECLARE THIS CHILD WILL HAVE THE GIFT OF SONG.

WHAT DO I SAY THERE?

CUUUUUUUT CUUUUUUUT

NOOOOOOO

I REPLY HOW?

NOTHING. YOU SAY NOTHING. YOU STAY LYING DOWN.

I DON'T SAY THANK YOU? ANYTHING?

NOTHING

WELL TRY ONE MORE TIME.

PUT SOME GUTS INTO IT, FOR CHRIST'S SAKE.

I DUNNO... THIS CHARACTER... I DON'T FEEL IT.

IT WOULD BE BETTER TO MAKE HER GIFTED AT COMEDY.

SILENCE. LIGHTS. ACTION. CAMERA. COME ON, COME ON.

I DON'T KNOW HOW TO SAY... IT'S NOT ME... I CAN'T RELATE TO IT. I THINK WE SHOULD RESHOOT THE SCENE FROM ANOTHER ANGLE.

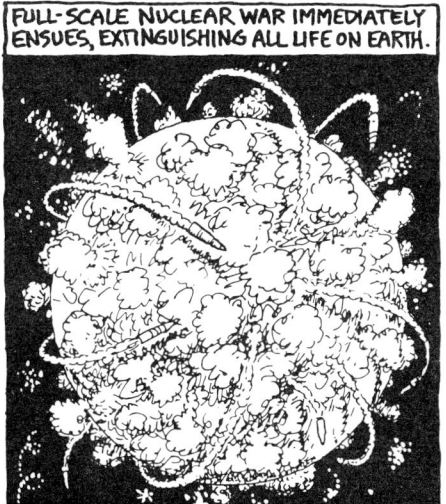

THE FABULOUS FURRY FREAK BROTHERS
by Gilbert Shelton

WELCOME TO OUR WELL-LOVED FRIEND

COPYRIGHT © 1985 RIPOFF PRESS, INC.

WOW! LOOK! THE PREMIER OF THE SOVIET UNION IS PAYING A VISIT!

THIS IS OUR CHANCE TO SEND HIM A MESSAGE!

WHAT DO WE WANT TO SAY?

END THE NUCLEAR WEAPONS BUILDUP? DOWN WITH SOVIET ADVENTURISM IN AFGHANISTAN?

STOP THE HUMAN RIGHTS VIOLATIONS?

FREE THE DISSENTERS IN THE GULAG?

HOW ABOUT THIS: DEAR MISTER PREMIER, IF YOU SEEK TRUE PEACE, IT MUST REQUIRE HUMILITY, NOT ARROGANCE; REMEMBER THE HELSINKI ACCORDS AND PROCEED WITH ALL DUE SPEED TOWARD A WORLD FREE FROM DESTRUCTIVE NUCLEAR WEAPONS, FREE OF AGGRESSIVE MILITARISM, AND FREE OF IMPERIALISM!

PERFECT!

NOW, HOW ARE WE GOING TO DELIVER IT TO HIM?

HEY, THE GUY DOESN'T SPEAK ENGLISH, Y'KNOW! LET ME TRANSLATE IT INTO RUSSIAN!

WHERE DID YOU LEARN TO SPEAK RUSSIAN, FREDDY?

REMEMBER, MY DAD LIVED IN WARSAW WHEN HE WAS A KID! HE PICKED IT UP FROM THE RED ARMY TROOPS!

IS THIS ALL? MY, RUSSIAN CERTAINLY IS A SUCCINCT LANGUAGE!

YEAH! NOW IT'S SHORT ENOUGH TO SPRAY PAINT IT ON THE SIDE OF A BUILDING!

THE NEXT DAY, AS THE SOVIET CHIEF OF STATE ROLLS THROUGH THE NEIGHBORHOOD ON HIS WAY TO THE AIRPORT...

GASP!!

ХУЙ С ТОБОЮ, ГОСПОДИН ПРЕМЬЕР-СЕКРЕТАРЬ, И ХУЙ С КОММУНИЗМОМ

"FUCK YOU, PREMIER, AND THE PIG YOU RODE IN ON"

FULL-SCALE NUCLEAR WAR IMMEDIATELY ENSUES, EXTINGUISHING ALL LIFE ON EARTH.

WHEW! WHAT AN UNTHINKABLE DREAM!

QUICK! HIDE THE SPRAY PAINT FROM FAT FREDDY!

35

THAT DROLL GROUP OF
WINE EXPERTS
WHO HANG OUT IN THE LITTLE PARK BEHIND THE CHURCH
WHAT DO YOU RECOMMEND FOR RUNNING SORES ALL OVER THE BODY?
I USUALLY APPLY SOME WINE, INTERNALLY!
GREAT IDEA! ANYBODY GOT ANY MONEY?
NAW, WE'LL HAVE TO GIVE SOME BLOOD.
COUNT ME OUT! I'VE ALREADY DONATED TWELVE TIMES THIS MONTH!
BESIDES, HE HAS AIDS!
THERE ARE ENOUGH DEPOSIT BOTTLES IN THIS BOX TO BUY A PINT OR SO!
IS A PINT ENOUGH TO CURE RUNNING SORES?
THIRTY TIMES ENOUGH.
HOW MUCH WOULD IT TAKE TO CURE AIDS?
WILL YOU QUIT ASKING ME FOR MEDICAL ADVICE? I'M NOT A DOCTOR, DAMMIT! NOT ANY MORE!
IT WOULD TAKE AT LEAST FIVE QUARTS.
YOU USED TO BE A DOCTOR?
YEAH, I WAS A SURGEON BEFORE I BECAME A WINE EXPERT BUT I GOT MY LICENSE REVOKED FOR HEROIN ADDICTION.
LET THAT BE A LESSON TO US ALL. STICK TO WINE!
LOOK! THERE ON THE GROUND A SIX DOLLAR BILL!
(EGAD! A CAREFULLY HAND-CRAFTED COUNTERFEIT SIX-DOLLAR BILL! THAT SORT OF THING IS WORTH HUNDREDS OF DOLLARS TO AN ART COLLECTOR!)
WHAT'LL IT BE, GENTLEMEN?
SIX QUARTS OF RED MOUNTAIN.
OH SHIT! THE BOTTOM DROPPED OUT OF THE BAG!
WINE
HUNDREDS OF WINE EXPERTS SUDDENLY ARRIVE OUT OF NOWHERE ATTRACTED BY THE BOUQUET.
ONE BOTTLE BROKE, BUT THERE ARE STILL FIVE QUARTS LEFT!
WHAT'LL WE DO? CURE ONE CASE OF AIDS, OR THREE HUNDRED CASES OF RUNNING SORES ALL OVER THE BODY?
WELL, AT LEAST I DON'T HAVE TO WORRY ABOUT RUNNING SORES ALL OVER THE BODY ANY LONGER.
SHUT UP AND PASS THE BOTTLE.
© 1985
G. SHELTON

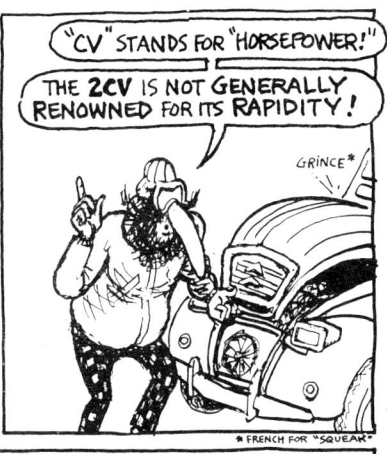

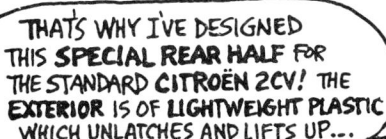

Gilbert Shelton's INTERNATIONAL MOTORING TIPS

COPYRIGHT © 1985 BY GILBERT SHELTON

No. 368

THIS IS MY CITROËN 2CV!

MANY CONSIDER THE 2CV THE WORLD'S MOST BEAUTIFUL CAR!

1980 CITROËN 2CV

"CV" STANDS FOR "HORSEPOWER!"

THE 2CV IS NOT GENERALLY RENOWNED FOR ITS RAPIDITY!

GRINCE*

*FRENCH FOR "SQUEAK"

THE 650 C.C., TWO-CYLINDER, FOUR-STROKE, AIR-COOLED ENGINE IS SUFFICIENT FOR CITY DRIVING...

ENGINE IS DOWN IN HERE SOMEPLACE

...BUT ON THE HIGHWAY IT HAS BARELY ENOUGH POWER TO PASS A LOADED CEMENT MIXER ON A HILL.

USING LEFT FOOT FOR ADDED POWER

SOME PEOPLE THINK THAT THE 2CV DRIVERS ARE DRIVING SLOWLY ON PURPOSE JUST TO ANNOY THEM, AND BEHAVE RUDELY.

ROAR   HONK   BEEEEEEP   FLASH FLASH   FLASH FLASH

THAT'S WHY I'VE DESIGNED THIS **SPECIAL REAR HALF** FOR THE STANDARD CITROËN 2CV! THE EXTERIOR IS OF LIGHTWEIGHT PLASTIC WHICH UNLATCHES AND LIFTS UP...

...REVEALING THE SUPERCHARGED 6.7-LITER **WILDEBEEST-COSWORTH V8** WHICH PRODUCES **950 HORSEPOWER** AT 7,500 R.P.M. ON METHANOL!

WHEN ANY OTHER MOTORIST SHOWS ME LACK OF RESPECT, I SWITCH ON THE REAR ENGINE AND OVERTAKE HIM.

WHENEVER I DRIVE THROUGH **PARIS** I HIRE A CORTÈGE OF **MUNICIPAL MOTO-POOPERSCOOPERS*** IN A TRIANGULAR FORMATION, TEN IN FRONT AND TEN BEHIND.

THEN, RELEASING FROM A PRESSURIZED TANK A SLIPPERY, FOUL-SMELLING MIXTURE OF USED MOTOR OIL AND LIQUID PIG FECES, I DISAPPEAR OVER THE HORIZON.

PROOT!   THE CRY OF THE ROAD-RUNNER   BEEP BEEP   ARGGGH!

*THE OFFICIAL PARIS SIDEWALK CLEANER, OR *RAMASSE-MERDE*: A SPECIAL YAMAHA WITH WATER SPRAY AND A LOWERING VACUUM CLEANER.

SLURP!   SUCK!

37

38

THAT AWFUL BORGIA POPE — His early years —

Eddie Campbell '86

AT INFANT SCHOOL HE WAS NOT THE QUICKEST TO LEARN

"My pencil is blunt"

"The other end, bambino"

"His pencil is blunt"

ONCE AS A CHILD HE LOCKED HIS MOTHER OUT OF THE HOUSE AND VIEWED HER ANGER FROM DIFFERENT WINDOWS

"Hee Hee"

THEN HE ROBBED THE FOOD MONEY WITHOUT CONSIDERING THAT HE WAS UNABLE TO GET OUT TO SPEND IT

VERY EARLY HE BEGAN TO DEVELOP THAT PARANOIA WHICH IS NATURAL TO PERSONS OF HIGH POSITION

"They are talking about me"

"His potato is peeled"

"ohh"

"They are saying horrid things behind my back"

"The soup's on but the gas ain't lit"

39

AS A YOUNG LAD HE HELD A TRUSTED POSITION AS HEAD ALTAR BOY AT THE CHURCH OF ST. EMILIO DA PONTE -
BURN THESE SURPLUS CONSECRATED HOSTS AND DISPOSE OF THIS HOLY WINE
YES FATHER
His crop has been harvested
It was here that he first showed his propensity to wickedness -
mm wotta jape
POP!
Hee Hee Sideways
NUM NUM
Now that really hit the spot
glub glub
Hee Hee Say, waiter - This blood is corked.

EVEN AS A PRE-PUBESCENT YOUTH HE USED DECEIT TO WIN THE FAVOURS OF WOMEN
OH, YOU HAVE SUCH HAIRY BALLS, RODRIGO.
The bus is full but there's Room on top
AND THOUGH HE WAS SLOW-WITTED HIS ANIMAL VITALITY AMUSED THEM
FETCH
WOOF
The window's open but the blinds are drawn
ON THE EVE OF HIS COMING OF AGE HIS MOTHER bought two ducklings FOR THE TRADITIONAL CELEBRATORY DINNER –
..AND A CURIOUS NOTION ENTERED HIS NOODLE.
oh what decadence it would be that I who have walked all day in the fierce heat..
SHOULD TAKE THESE DUCKS FROM THE NICE COOL LARDER..
..AND WEAR THEM AS SLIPPERS.

THLOOP THLOOP

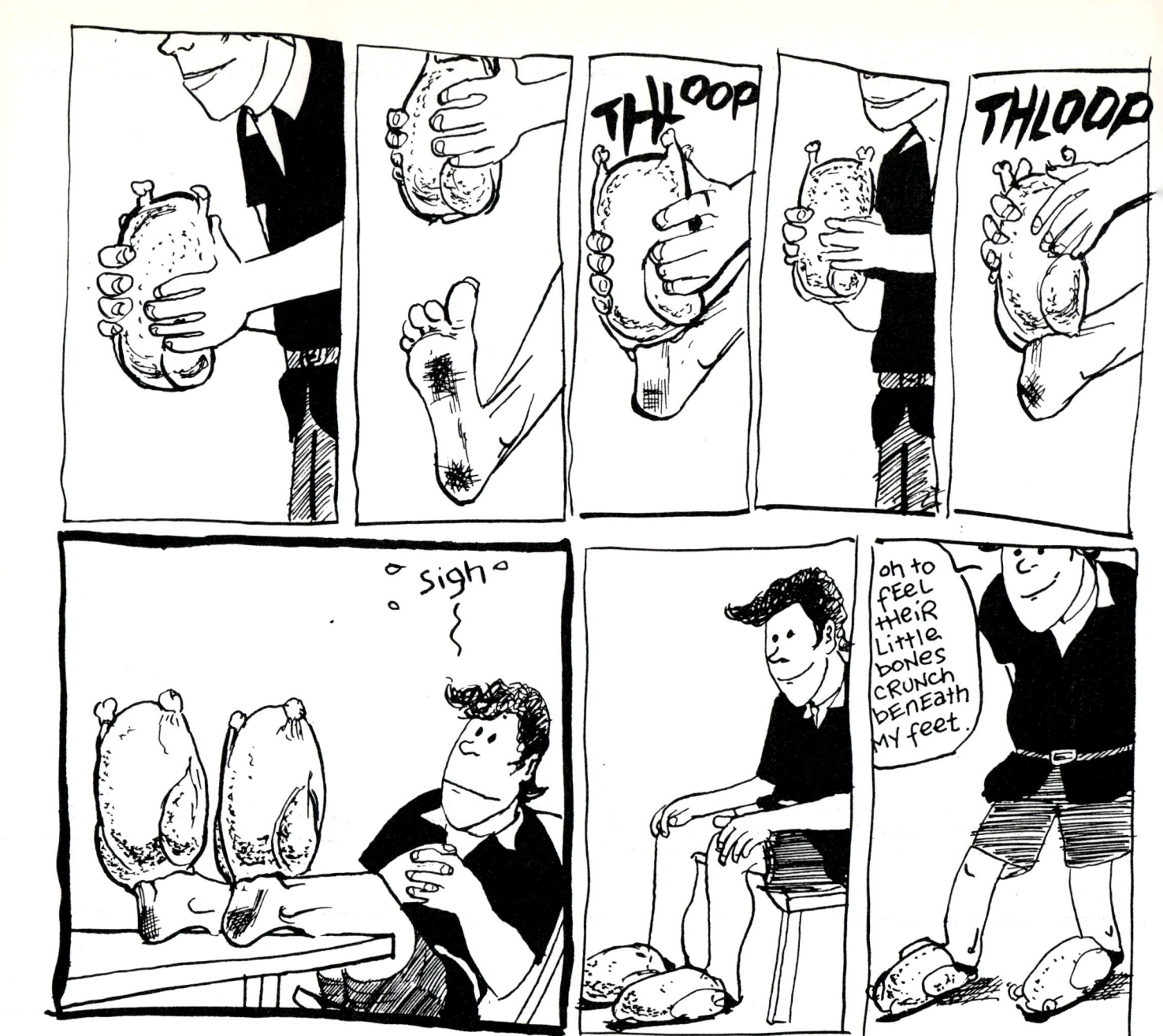

°sigh°

oh to feel their little bones crunch beneath my feet.

AND LATER IN HIS TIME OF GREATNESS HE WOULD REMEMBER THAT DINNER WITH AMUSEMENT.

YUK YUK

Mama, have I got a wing?

Mama, have I got the right foot or the left foot?

His banana is split

Ah, you talka nonsense Rodrigo. Eata you dinner.

YOU HAVE JUST BEEN READING *GREAT TEDDYBOYS THROUGH HISTORY* PART ONE. NEXT WEEK'S TEDDY BOY: COLONEL GADAFI — Eddie Campbell

CALCULUS CAT
By Hunt Emerson

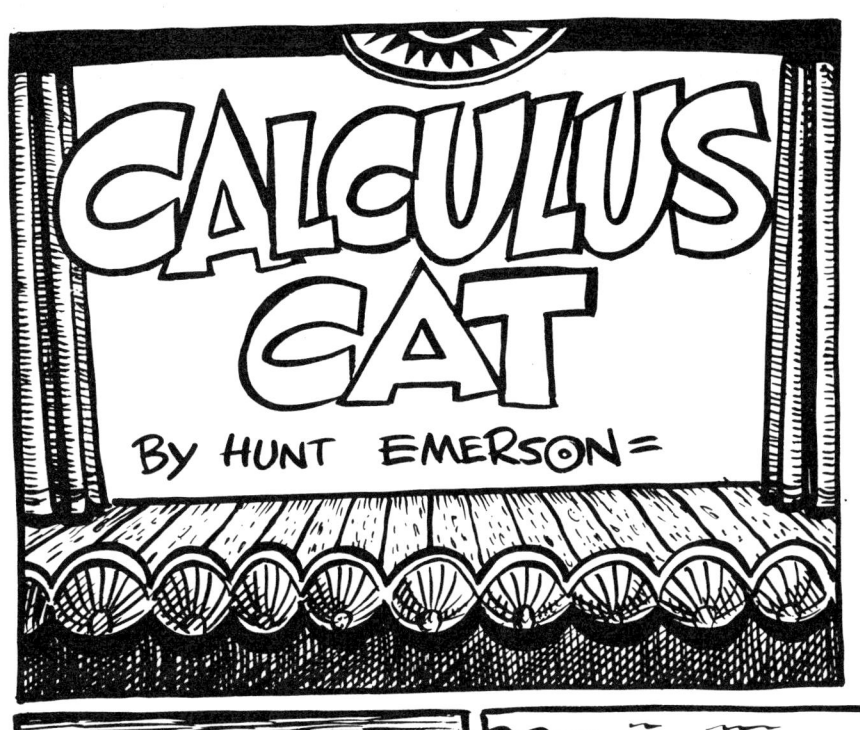

HOME!
C. CAT ESQ.

43

CAT
Sigh...
CLIK
CAT
GOOD EVENING, BOSS.
Munch Chomp... GOOD EVENING TEEVEE! Munch
CHOMP GOBBLE
SLURP
CAT
NOW, HERE WE GO WITH THIS EVENINGS...
HEL-LO! WHO CAN THAT BE?
KNOCKNOCKNOCKNOCKNOCKNOCKNOCK
URP!
CAT
THE SEA!!!
HAVE YOU SEEN IT??! HAVE YOU SEEN THE SEA?!?
...IT MUST BE ROUND HERE SOMEWHERE!!... ...THE SEA...

"...I MUST FIND THE SEA!..."

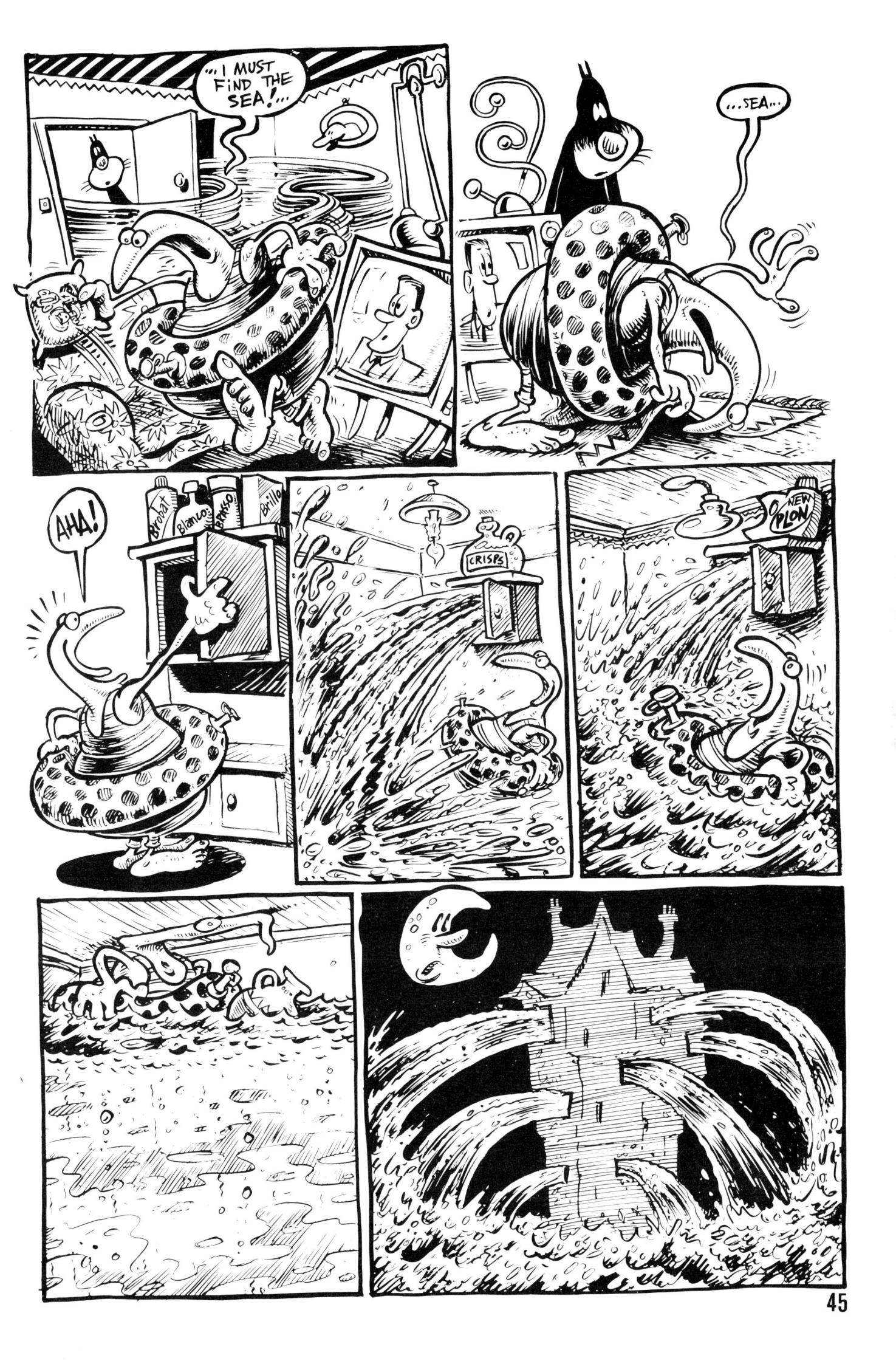

"...SEA..."

AHA!

"THE SEA!"

"OH, **THAT** SEA.... IS IT YOURS? IT WAS IN THAT CUPBOARD WHEN I MOVED INTO THIS FLAT!.."

"WHAT SEA IS IT?"

BLOOSH!

SLURP
TP-TP-TP-TP... HMM!- ENGLISH CHANNEL 1956!
I SAY, I'M SORRY-DID I DISTURB YOU?
NO-I WAS WATCHIN' THE TELLY!
WHAT'S ON?
DUNNO! T.V.?- WHAT'S ON?
...er... "THE ADDAMS FAMILY!"
OH, GREAT!
TV TIMES
BUT FIRST- A COMMERCIAL BREAK....
SETTLE SETTLE SETTLE
"SKWEEKY WEETS" ARE THE SKWEEKY WEETY WEET SKWEEKS FOR ME!
SPLISH SPLOSH
Their house is a museyum When people come to seeyum When people is a screeyum- It really is a The Addams Family!
LAP LAP LAP
PURR PURR
THE END.

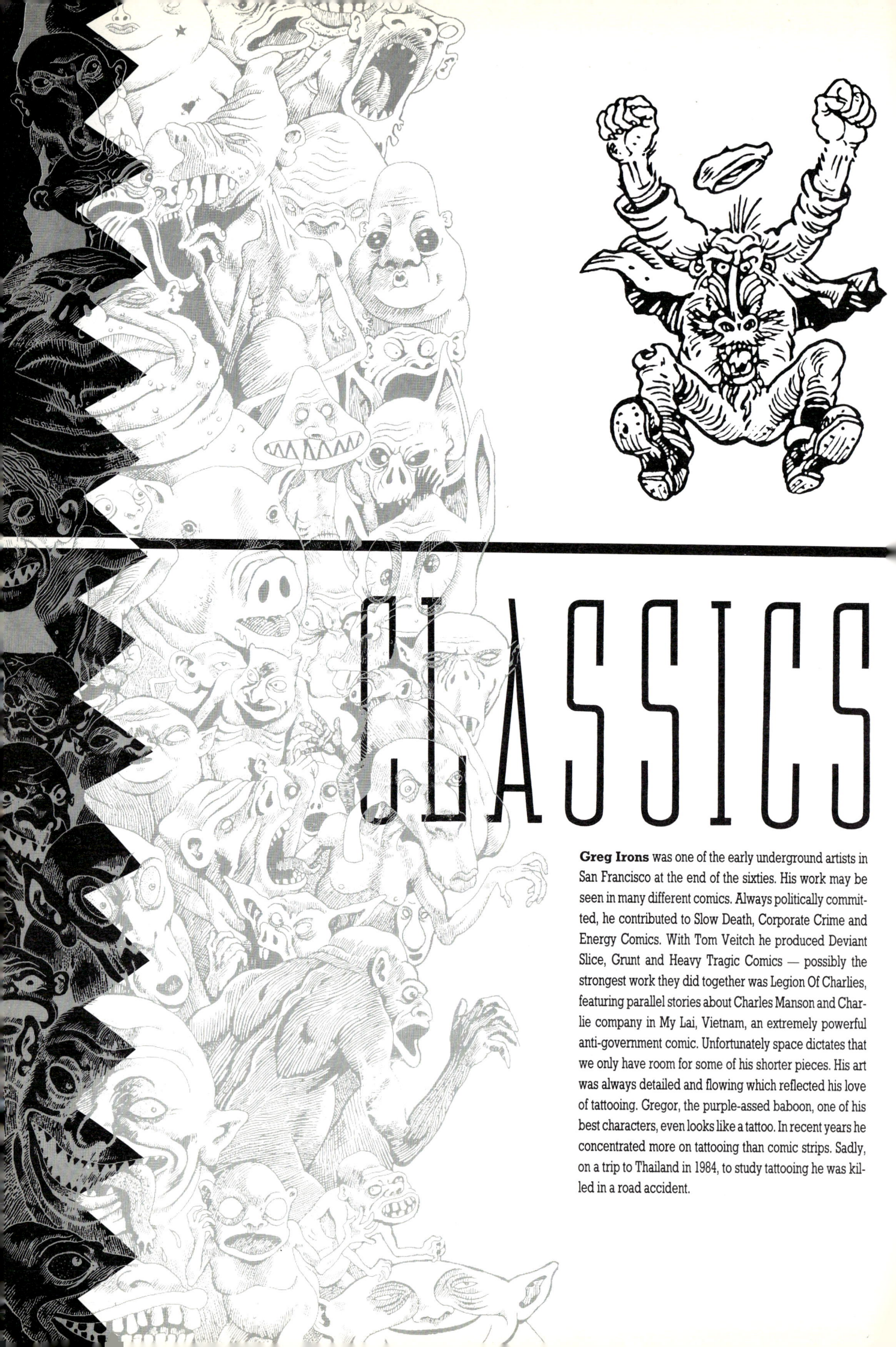

CLASSICS

Greg Irons was one of the early underground artists in San Francisco at the end of the sixties. His work may be seen in many different comics. Always politically committed, he contributed to Slow Death, Corporate Crime and Energy Comics. With Tom Veitch he produced Deviant Slice, Grunt and Heavy Tragic Comics — possibly the strongest work they did together was Legion Of Charlies, featuring parallel stories about Charles Manson and Charlie company in My Lai, Vietnam, an extremely powerful anti-government comic. Unfortunately space dictates that we only have room for some of his shorter pieces. His art was always detailed and flowing which reflected his love of tattooing. Gregor, the purple-assed baboon, one of his best characters, even looks like a tattoo. In recent years he concentrated more on tattooing than comic strips. Sadly, on a trip to Thailand in 1984, to study tattooing he was killed in a road accident.

A PORTRAIT OF THE ARTEEST
AS A BURNT BABOON
WHY NOT STEP DOWN TO TO MY STUDIO AND I'LL SHOW YOU MY ETCHINGS..
GREGOR IS IN TRAINING ..PREPARING FOR A DIFFICULT ASSIGNMENT
LOOK OUT
OOPS
OOF!
KLUNK
THUD
BONK
CRASH
OW
ARGH
THUNK
BUMF
BONK
BONK
AK OUCH OW OOF EEE OW OW OW OW OW
THUMPA THUMPA THUMPA THUM THU TH T
TINK
TINK
CRASH!
BONK
BEHOLD THE GREAT ARTEEST. UP AND AT 'EM, CHAMP.
JUST RESTING..
HE CAN'T SEEM TO WORK UNTIL HE'S DRIVEN HIMSELF CRAZY..
SHIT. NOT CRAZY.
..AND CRAZY IS FUN FUN FUN..
UNFORTUNATELY IT'S TAKEN IT'S TOLL ON THE TEMPLE OF HIS SOUL..
HERE..GET "CREATIVE" OL' BUDDY..
CIGARETTES AND WHISKEY.. CALM MY SHAKING HAND..
GREGOR'S TRIED IT STRAIGHT..WITHOUT MUCH SUCCESS.
AHEM..NOTE THE STIPPLING EFFECT..
DR. WIRTHAM'S #5 COMIX & STORIES
I HATE IT!
SMEK!

GREGOR WORKS BEST UNDER STRESS..
SHITFUCK GODDAM TRASH SHIT GIMME A FUCKING BEER!
..GOOD THING TOO.. DEADLINE IS LAST WEEK..
SO NOW HE'S PREPARING TO MEET HIS OBLIGATIONS..
..ANYTHING TO AMUSE THE KIDS!
INSPIRATION
GREGOR HAS ALWAYS HAD A FLAIR FOR THE DRAM-ATIC.
PUNCH IT, GREGOR. FEED MEDIA AND IT WILL FEED YOU.. IF IT DOESN'T EAT YOU UP.
..IT IS A VIOLENT GOD WHICH REQUIRES SACRIFICE. GOT TO STRUGGLE GOT TO BLEED. GOT TO...
ZIP!
YAAARGH!
GOUGH MAN, GOUGH. YOU CAN HACK IT, HACK.
..LAST WE HEARD, GREGOR HAD ABANDONED THE BIG-TIME IN PURSUIT OF "FINE ART"..
TATTOOING
YOU MUST BE 21 TO OBTAIN OUR SERVICES
HOW YOU SPELLIN "CAROL"?
© 1980 Irons
DRAWN WITH ACTUAL BLOOD

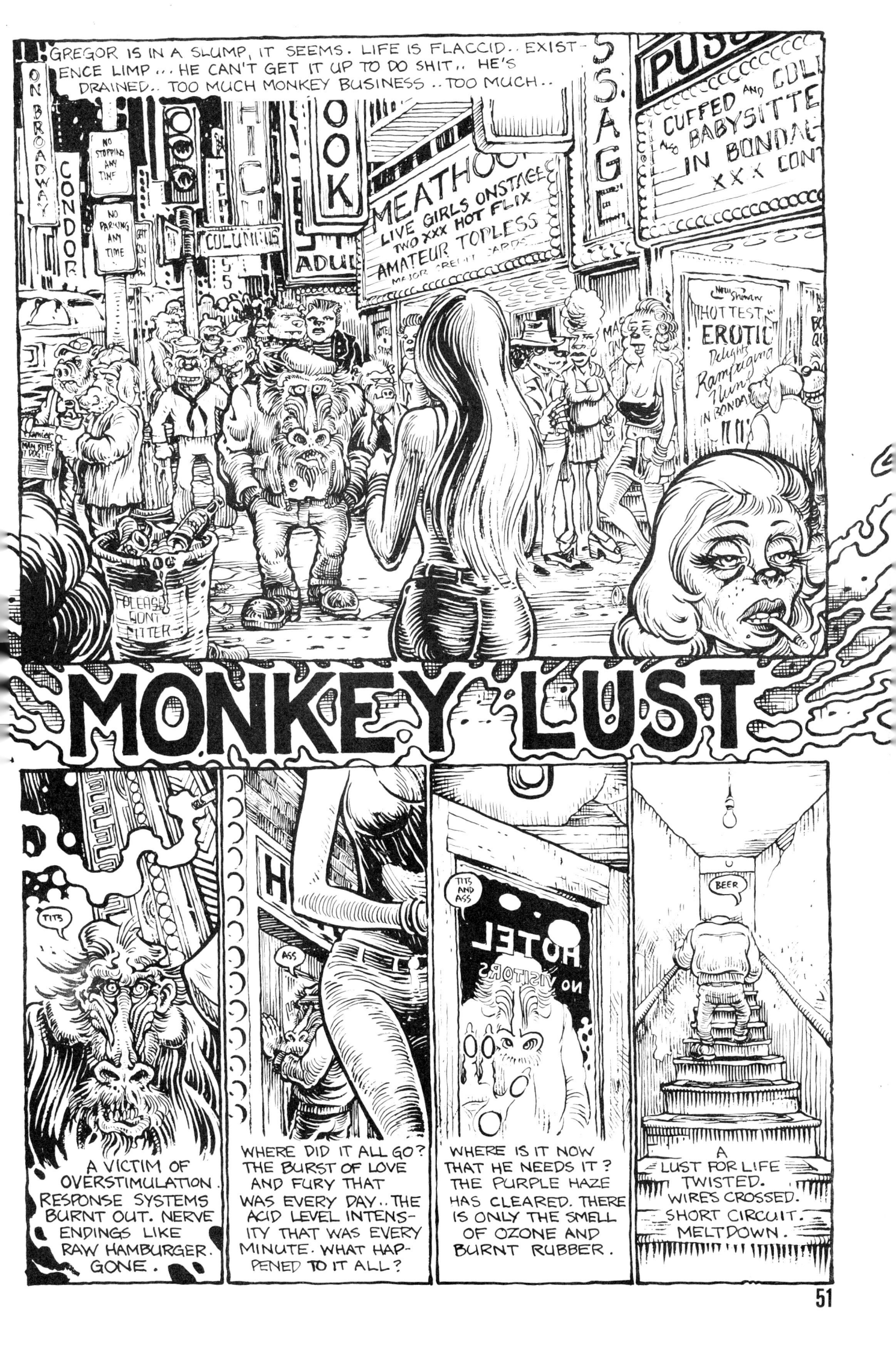

GREGOR IS IN A SLUMP, IT SEEMS. LIFE IS FLACCID. EXISTENCE LIMP... HE CAN'T GET IT UP TO DO SHIT. HE'S DRAINED. TOO MUCH MONKEY BUSINESS... TOO MUCH..

MONKEY LUST

A VICTIM OF OVERSTIMULATION. RESPONSE SYSTEMS BURNT OUT. NERVE ENDINGS LIKE RAW HAMBURGER. GONE.

WHERE DID IT ALL GO? THE BURST OF LOVE AND FURY THAT WAS EVERY DAY... THE ACID LEVEL INTENSITY THAT WAS EVERY MINUTE. WHAT HAPPENED TO IT ALL?

WHERE IS IT NOW THAT HE NEEDS IT? THE PURPLE HAZE HAS CLEARED. THERE IS ONLY THE SMELL OF OZONE AND BURNT RUBBER.

A LUST FOR LIFE TWISTED. WIRES CROSSED. SHORT CIRCUIT. MELTDOWN.

Panel 1	Panel 2	Panel 3

Panel 1: THERE'S SO MUCH TO CHOOSE FROM.. AND SO FEW CHOICES. HE'S FOUNDERING IN A POOL ON THE MUDFLATS. THE RECEEDING TIDE HAS LEFT HIM AWASH IN A STINKING, SLIMEY HOLE..
BLUB

Panel 2: BUT WHAT'S THAT SMELL LIKE FISH, OH BABY?

Panel 3: HOW MANY TIMES DOES HE HAVE TO GO THRU THIS SHIT? CERTAINLY A "NORMAL" RELATIONSHIP IS OUT OF THE QUESTION..
SPLAT!

Panel 4: THE MOST HE HOPES FOR IS MOMENTARY TITILLATION. SOMETHING HE CAN FOCUS ON FOR TEN SECONDS OR LESS... THE SOOTHING DRONE OF THE TV SET WILL WASH HIS CHARRED PSYCHE CLEAN. NO FEELING... NO PAIN.
- THE ANGELS HIT THE STREET AS WORKING GIRLS TONIGHT ON CHAR ≶KLIK≶
- ANGIE POSES AS A HOOKER TO TRY TO CATCH A RAPIST LATENIGHT ON THE BIG..≶KLIK≶
- ..I LOVE YOU, TOO, ANN..
- NURSE JONES, I WANT TO PROPOSITION YOU.. WHAT? RIGHT HERE IN THIS ≶KLICK≶
- ..OK BABY, DROP IT ≶KLIK≶
- .SHOW US YOUR LEGS, AMERICA..≶KLICK≶
- WRRR...

Panel 5: THE MOST POSITIVE FUTURE HE CAN CONJURE IS A LIFE FREE OF IRRITATION..
OH MR. JOHNSON. IT'S THESE ITCHING, BURNING TISSUES.. YOU KNOW.. ≶KLICK≶

Panel 6: BUT THE AIR WAVES ARE FULL OF BAD VIBRATIONS.. ELECTROMAGNETIC ICONS ARE EVERYWHERE.
..SMOOTH..SLEEK.. I LOVE IT!
BELCH!

Panel 7: THE MEDIA IS OUR NEW RELIGION.. OUR GODDESSES ARE AIRBRUSHED FOLDOUTS.. OUR GODS ARE MARLBORO SMOKING OLYMPIANS.. FOOTBALL COWBOYS.. WHITE TOOTHED FLASHES OF MEAT BLAZING IN A QUICK FLIRT WITH GLORY..
- THIS TROJAN OFFENSE HAS GOT THE DEEP PENITRATION, CLINT!
- MY HEART IS YOURS, BO BABY.. AS FOR YOU, BITCH, WIPE THAT FUCKING GRIN OFF YOUR FACE OR I'LL LINE THE GARBAGE CAN WITH YOU!

52

..AN AGING APE HOPELESSLY TANGLED UP IN THE YOUTH CULTURE... HOO BOY!

HIS DESTINY SHAPED BY HIS CONDITIONING.
PUFF PANT GASP.

THE NET PRODUCT PACKAGED UP AND SOLD TO HIM IN NICKLE BAGS BY THE PUSHER MAN.
TAKE YOU TO FUNKY TOWN!

..AND HE'S BOUGHT IT IN SPITE OF HIMSELF. NO WONDER HE'S BURNT OUT. CAPS ON YOUR TEETH AND HAIR IMPLANTS AREN'T GONNA HELP VERY MUCH.
BAD, HUH?
GREGOR'S NEWEST VIRILE IMAGE.

HIS COMPLICATED EXISTENCE IS THE DANCE OF A DISCARDED CIGARETTE PACKAGE BLOWING IN THE GUTTER.

A CRUMPLED, USELESS REMINDER OF A LIFE ALREADY BURNED.. OH, WELL.. GET OUT THERE AND FIGHT AND FUCK, GREGOR.
HI THERE! WANT A "DATE"?
HOW MUCH?

HIS ACTIONS ARE PUPPET RAVINGS.. NASTY MANIFESTATIONS OF THE PATTERNING DESIGNED TO ADVANCE HIS GENETIC CODE INTO INFINITY...
HOWDY DOODY, BEAUTIFUL! PERHAPS YOU'D CARE TO INDULGE IN A LITTLE ORANGATANGADINGDONG?
I AM BUT A HUSK FOR MY SEED.
WHY DON'T YOU TAKE YOUR FILTHY PAW OFF ME BEFORE I GET MY HUSBAND TO BREAK YOUR ARMS.

YOUR REASON FOR LIVING ENDED WITH A SPURT 15 YEARS AGO, GREGOR.
SPURT
INSTEAD OF GETTING BETTER, IT'S GOTTEN WORSE.

..MUST BE SOMETHING GOOD ON TV... BUT EACH SWEET YOUNG THING CAUSES ANOTHER JOLT TO SURGE THROUGH HIS USELESS MEMORY BANKS.. A SPONTANEOUS FLASH REACTION DOWN THRU THE TWISTED WRECKAGE OF HIS DNA CHAINS. HE'S BECOME A PIMP FOR HIS OWN CHROMOSOMES.
OH MY GOD! SHE GONNA PEAK OUT ANY SECOND!

53

Panel 1	Panel 2	Panel 3
HE'S A ROBOT.. DESTINED TO REPEAT OVER AND OVER HIS LITTLE DANCE OF DEATH "I AM A MECHANICAL BOY."	HE'S WIRED IN.. TWITCHING LIKE THE ELECTRICUTED MAN.. ALREADY DEAD BUT GIVEN ANOTHER HIT OF JUICE JUST TO BE SURE.. ...TANTRIC BOOGIE...	YOU'VE ALREADY GIVEN IT YOUR BEST SHOT, GREGOR. THE REST IS JUST A BAD JOKE.. A NIGHTMARE IN ONE ACT TO BE PLAYED UNTIL YOUR TIMELY END.

..EVEN THEN, THE PURGATORY OF FIERY VULVAS AWAITS..

WAAAH! POP

WHA.. POP

OH SHIT! I GOT A HOT DATE IN TWENTY MINUTES!

LATER REMEMBER, GREGOR, YOU ARE WHAT YOU EAT.

?

GET DOWN, BIG BOY!

© 1980 G. Irons

54

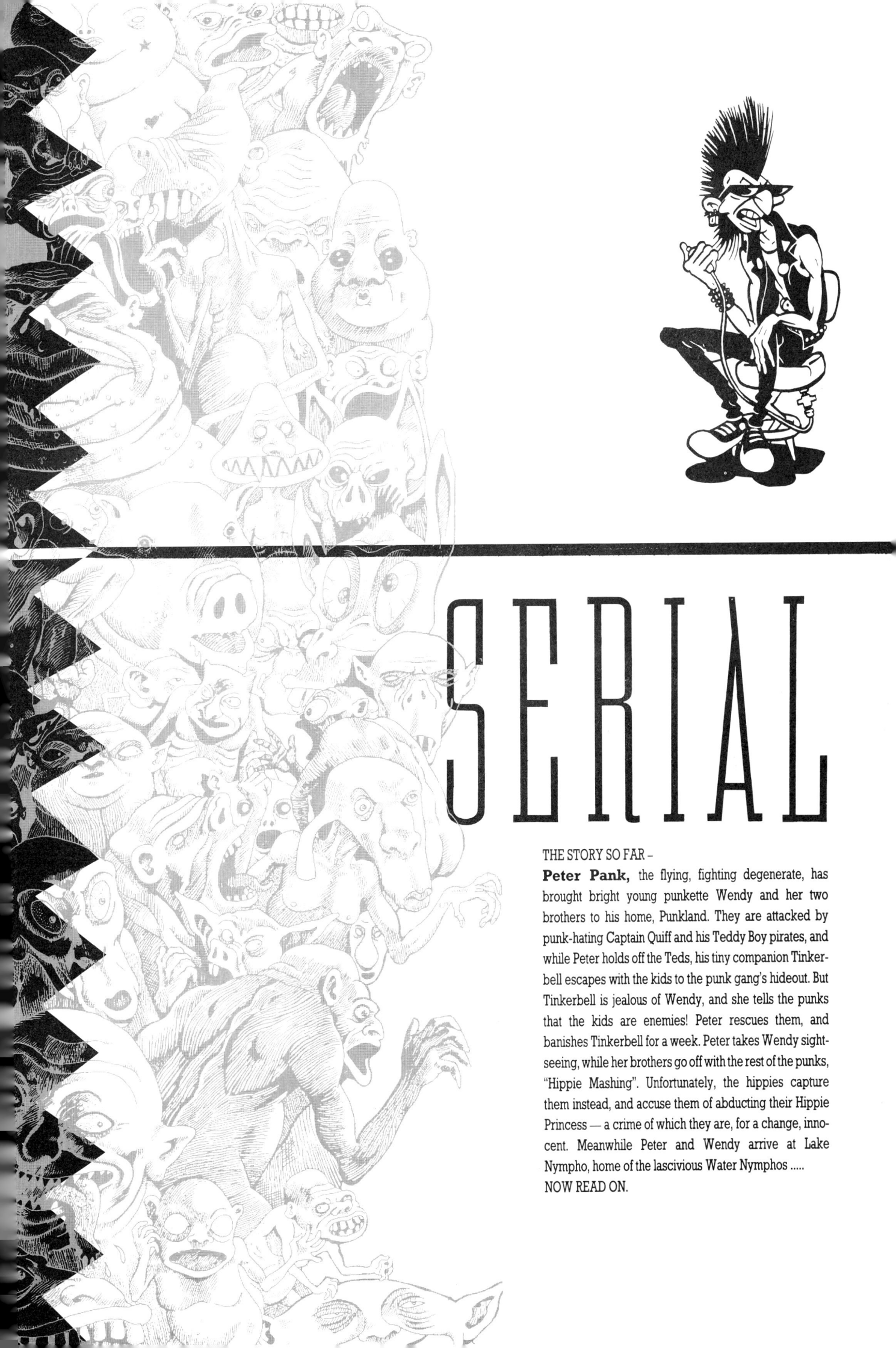

SERIAL

THE STORY SO FAR –

Peter Pank, the flying, fighting degenerate, has brought bright young punkette Wendy and her two brothers to his home, Punkland. They are attacked by punk-hating Captain Quiff and his Teddy Boy pirates, and while Peter holds off the Teds, his tiny companion Tinkerbell escapes with the kids to the punk gang's hideout. But Tinkerbell is jealous of Wendy, and she tells the punks that the kids are enemies! Peter rescues them, and banishes Tinkerbell for a week. Peter takes Wendy sightseeing, while her brothers go off with the rest of the punks, "Hippie Mashing". Unfortunately, the hippies capture them instead, and accuse them of abducting their Hippie Princess — a crime of which they are, for a change, innocent. Meanwhile Peter and Wendy arrive at Lake Nympho, home of the lascivious Water Nymphos .....
NOW READ ON.

max
Peter Pank
TOPOGRAPHIC SUMMARY OF THE SITUATION
BLACK OCEAN
DEATH ROCK
JOHN O'GROATS
CAPTAIN QUIFF HEADING TOWARDS DEATH ROCK WITH A PRISONER
DEATH COAST
VIRGIN JUNGLE (PROBABLY INHABITED BY SAVAGES AND DINOSAURS)
LAKE NYMPHO (PETER AND WENDY ARE HERE)
DEATH VALLEY
THE NYMPHOS CAVES
SHARKS ALWAYS SCROUNGING.
SECRET BAY OF CAPTAIN QUIFF AND HIS TEDS
BRIGHTON BEACH (SURFING ZONE)
HIGH ESTUARY
CIMERIA
PETER'S SECRET CAMP (NO ONE HOME)
River Thames!
Ben Frost 1499m
BLACK MOUNTAINS
SPOOKY ISLAND
MYSTERIOUS TOWER
THE MOSSY FOREST
N.
LAND'S END
TINKERBELL, PISSED OFF WITH PETER, IS DOSSING IN THIS AREA SOMEWHERE.
HIPPIE COMMUNE (PETER'S PUNK PALS AND THE BRATS ARE PRISONERS, ACCUSED OF KIDNAPPING THE HIPPIE PRINCESS)
DESERT
MEGALITHIC REMAINS
SWAMPS
MARIJUANA FOREST
COSTA DEL SOL
LOW ESTUARY
PUNKLAND
Scale - 1:250.000
CLIFFS (not RICHARDS)
NUDE BEACH!
APPROVED BY NATIONAL GEOGRAPHIC MAGAZINE 1983
OI-OI! THIS IS MY FRIEND, WENDY!
OH! ISN'T SHE LOVELY!!
WHAT A CUTIE!!
COME FOR A SWIM, WENDY - THE WATER'S DELICIOUS!
THE SNOT STILL LIVES
OI! LEAVE OFF!
COME ON, PETER - WE ONLY WANNA PLAY!
YEAH!!
ANOTHER TIME! NOW WE'VE GOTTA... uh?!
'EAR THAT? QUIFF MUST BE ABOUT!
HE SOUNDS HAPPY! THAT CAN ONLY MEAN ONE OF HIS EVIL SCHEMES HAS WORKED!
Don't step on my Blue Suede Shoes, ya basstid...
C'MON, WENDY, LET'S GO AND SPY ON THE FILTHY CROW!
WHAT A SWINE! HE JUST WANTS HER FIRST!
OOOH - SHE'S REALLY GOT ME GOING! IMAGINE WHAT WE COULD GET UP TO WITH HER!
WHY DON'T WE HIJACK HER AND TAKE HER TO OUR CAVE?!

HOLY SNOT! HE'S GOT THE HIPPY PRINCESS AND HE'S TAKIN' HER TO DEATH ROCK! WHAT'S THAT WANKER GOT IN MIND?!

COME ON, LITTLE PRINCESS - JUST TELL ME WHERE PETER'S HIDEOUT IS AND I'LL LET YOU GO!

NEVER!!

OK, THEN, I'LL GIVE MY CREW A SURPRISE PARTY! HEHHEH...

TCHA! WOULDN'T BE THE FIRST TIME I'VE SCREWED THAT LOT!

YOU FUCKIN' SLAG! LET'S SEE IF YOU HAVE AS GOOD A TIME WITH THE SHARKS AS YOU DO WITH MY MEN! NOW, WHERE'S.....

LOOKIN' FOR SOMEONE, QUIFF?!

WHAT QUIFF SEES FREEZES HIS BLOOD....

THE SAVAGE SWORD OF **PETER PANK** *The Barbarian!*

THE PIRATE TEDDYBOY REACTS SWIFTLY...

CRETIN! YOU HAD YOUR CHANCE AND YOU BLEW IT - NOW I'M GONNA CUT YOU LIKE THE SAVAGE YOU ARE!!

...AND THE SHINING STEEL STARTS A DANCE MACABRE!

TWO SAVAGE GIANTS THIRSTY FOR EACH OTHERS' BLOOD...

...BUT THE HUGE KITCHEN KNIFE IS USELESS AGAINST THE SKILL WITH WHICH CAP'N QUIFF USES HIS FLICK KNIFE! COCINA POCO PUEDE CONTRA LA HABILIDAD CON QUE EL CAPITAN DE LOS ROCKERS MANEJA LA AUTOMÁTICA

NEVERTHELESS, A WILD SWING BY PETER DISARMS HIS ENEMY!

QUIFF'S EYES BURN AS HE ZEROS IN ON PETER'S HEART....

Hur Hur Hur..!!

TED OVER BOARD!!!

BUT PETER'S A DIRTY CHEAT, AND DOESN'T GIVE A SHIT ABOUT HONOUR WHEN IT COMES TO USING HIS FLYING POWERS.....

STAY COOL, CAPTAIN, MAN! WE'RE COMIN'!!
UAAAAARGH! BALLS TO COOL!! GET ME OUTA HERE!!!
CAROL
HMM! THINGS IS LOOKIN' UGLY! NO TIME TO WASTE, PRINCESS!
OH, PETER! IT'S BEEN A LONG TIME!
THE SMELL OF PETER'S SWEAT MAKES THE PRINCESS FEEL HORNY, (ODD GIRL...)
TAKE ME TO YOUR CAVE, PETER!
NO WAY! I'M TAKIN' YOU BACK TO YOUR HIPPIES....BUT...er... IT'S A LONG WAY BACK...heh...

Panel 1:
"HOLD TIGHT, BABY...HurHurrr!!"

Panel 2:
"HURRY UP CAPTAIN!!"
"GET BACK FISH FACE!"

Panel 3:
"BRRRR!! FLYING SWINE...I'LL GET EVEN WITH YOU! NO HOLDS BARRED FROM NOW ON! FIND ME TINKERBELL!"

Panel 4:
THE EXCITEMENT OF THE FIGHT, AND THE BIGGEST TITS ON THE ISLAND MAKE PETER FORGET ABOUT WENDY FOR THE MOMENT...HE DOESN'T NOTICE HER LAGGING BEHIND....

"=gasp= I CAN'T FLY ANY FURTHER!"

Panel 5:
"=Sniff= HE...HE IGNORED ME! I WONDER WHAT'S HAPPENED TO MY LITTLE BROTHERS... AND WHERE THE HELL AM I?"

Panel 6:
"GRAB HER, GIRLS!"
"EH?"
"GOTCHA!!"

AAAAAAH!!
OH-HO! A WILD LITTLE PUSSYCAT, EH?
UGH!!
......
WE'LL TAME YOU! YOU'LL LEARN TO OBEY! GIVE ME A ROPE!
HEEELLP PETER!
TO THE CAVES!
SQUAWK AS MUCH AS YOU LIKE, DARLIN'- PETER WON'T HEAR YOU- HE'S OTHERW: ENGAGED!!
TO BE SURE, PETER WAS QUITE OBLIVIOUS...
SSLURP!!
OH PETER! YOU'RE FANTASTIC!!
MMM...THIS LOOKS A BIT DULL... NEEDS BRIGHTENIN' UP A BIT, I THINK..
COO! WOT'S DIS, DEN?
shlup shlup
gloop glab
slurp slurp!
OOOH! YESSS....GO ON...., OOOO....YES... NOW....YESSSS!!!...
SUDDENLY...
WENDY!! OH MY GAWD!!
2,!! HEY...WHAT THE FUCK..?! I WAS JUST ABOUT TO COOOMEEA!
...SO WAS PETER!
UUUUH!!
HIS ORGASM LEAVES DAZED FOR AN INSTANT, BUT HE REGAINS CONTROL AND TAKES A DIVE...TO HELL.....

MEANWHILE, AT THE HIPPIE COMMUNE, THINGS ARE GETTING HOT...
KILL MAIM DESTROY
THE END IS NIGH, PUNKS! THE SUN IS SETTING!!
ANY LAST WISHES? Heheh...
LOOK UP THERE!!
I WANT MY SISTER!!
I WANT MY GLUE!!
THE HIPPIES LOCP IN HORROR...DOS...
AAAAAAAH!!
BUT PETER ARRIVES IN TIME TO SAVE HER FROM A NASTY FATE!...
OOOOH!!
?!!
....BUT NOT FROM A MIGHTY ORGASM! THE PRINCESS DIGS THRILLS!
FWWOOOAARR!! IMPALED ALIVE! Hurhur hurhur!
WOTS HAPPNIN?
WENDY!
UUUUUHH!!
NOT THE TRIBE'S WITCH DOCTOR, BUT THE PRINCESS' BOYFRIEND....
UH...AAAH!! OH GOD! WHAT AN ORGASM!! PETER, YOU'RE REALLY FAR OUT, MAAAAAN....
CRASH!
AAH!!
BRING THE BASTARD HERE!!!

SHIT! IT'S MY FATHER!
NO, DADDY, WAIT! PETER SAVED ME FROM THE ROCKERS! THEY HIJACKED ME!
WOSS 'APPNIN'?!
TCHAAH! I'D 'AVE LET 'ER FALL!!
HEY, PEETEERR!! GET US OUT OF HERE!!
WHERE'S WENDY?!
OK, HIPPIES! THIS SEZ LET MY MATES GO, OR ELSE!
DADDY - LET THE BOYS GO! THEY'RE MY FRIENDS!!
GRRR - OK, LET THEM FREE....
AND YOU! PUT YOUR KNICKERS ON!
C'MON, LET US GO.... FARKIN' 'IPPIES....!!!
GRRRR!!
WHERE'S WENDY?
WHO'S WENDY?
SHIT! WENDY!...
THE FESTIVAL OF THE FULL MOON GETS INTO FULL SWING......
WHAT HAVE YOU DONE WITH MY SISTER?
YOU WANTED A PARTY, EH HIPPIE? WELL NOW YOU GOT ONE! Haah!
PETER! WHERE ARE YOU GOING? WAIT!
BLIMEY!
WHO'S GOT ME GLUE?
— HOW WILL THE HIPPIES STAND UP TO A PUNK TRASHING?
— IS PETER TOO LATE TO SAVE WENDY'S INNOCENCE??
— AND WHAT ABOUT CAPTAIN QUIFF? BOY - IS HE MAD!?!
~ Don't miss next issue!

KNOCKABOUT number 11
Glacial glamour & refrigerated rabbits
295 x 210mm Paperback
ISBN 0 86166 037 4
£4.50 inc. postage

OPIUM
Daniel Torres
295 x 210mm. Paperback
ISBN 0 86166 047 1
£5.50 inc. postage

FREAK BROTHERS collection one
The Early Years
295 x 210mm. Paperback
ISBN 0 86166 040 4
£5.50 inc. postage

JAZZ FUNNIES
Hunt Emerson
295 x 210mm Paperback
ISBN 0 86166 046 3
£5.00 inc. postage

Send for free illustrated catalogue of American imported comics and the best of Knockabout Publications. Plus T-shirts, badges and postcards.

KNOCKABOUT, UNIT 6a, 10 ACKLAM ROAD, LONDON W10 5QZ

KNOCKABOUT